The Holy Grail of Gluten Free,

Dairy Free, Yeast Free,

Rice Free, Bean Free,

Almost Entirely

Soy Free...

Dawn Schlosser

On the cover: Chalice, circa 1390 by Pizino, Musée des Beaux-Arts de Lyon.
Photo of Chalice © 2010 Marie-Lan Nguyen

Frame Photos, pp. 16, 31 and 75 © EKDuncan http://eveyd.deviantart.com

Many thanks to my proofreaders, Elizabeth, Serena, and Mom, and to
Mark, who cleaned my kitchen.

First Edition

ISBN: 1-484046-70-6

ISBN-13: 978-1-484046-70-8

Most Humble Table of Contents

Scattered Words of Wisdom

Measuring

Measurements are crucial. Baking is more like chemistry than cooking, and poor measurements can completely alter your results. I cannot overstate this. Don't guess, measure. Level measuring cups and spoons, weigh dry ingredients whenever possible, and find a good, read from above, liquid measuring cup with markings down to ¼ C/60mL.

To speed up measuring and weighing ingredients, set the sifter into the dry bowl and the bowl onto the scale. You can now measure your flours straight into the sifter! Just don't forget to tare/zero out the scale.

Keep a spoon handy while weighing out dry ingredients. That way, if you get a little over excited and pour too heavily, you can scoop some back out.

For evenly sized cupcakes and muffins, I like to use a ¼ C measuring cup to scoop the batter into the muffin tins. It's usually exactly the right amount for each cupcake/muffin, and you're sure to get a pretty uniform amount in each cup.

Prep Tips

For cakes, cupcakes and muffins it is important to get the batter into the pans as soon as it is mixed together or you will lose rise. Then, if for some reason you can't bake them immediately, the batter filled pans can be covered and popped into the fridge until time to bake them, usually with little to no damage.

For delicate cut-out cookie and pie crust doughs, rolling them out onto or between silicone baking mats is an awesome cheat. The mats can be gently rolled back away from more fragile recipes, releasing them easily and saving the shapes, and the mats won't crease or crinkle like parchment or waxed paper.

Always use a scraper to scrape out your bowls! It's quick and easy, keeps your measurements right, and you won't waste expensive ingredients by washing them down the sink.

I hate the unclean feeling of dough stuck to my hands. To scrub it off quickly, wash with a tsp of salt instead of soap. The mild abrasion works wonders. This trick is also great to use after painting.

Making Ahead

For quick cookies, you can freeze these doughs for 1-2 months, then bake a few up whenever the cravings strike.

Cookie recipes that freeze well:

To always have something ready to eat, bake up a lot of the recipes that freeze well and tuck them into the freezer for later!

Recipes that freeze especially well:

For super fast wraps, make up the batter for these crêpes ahead and keep it covered in your fridge. Whisk it back together and make a couple whenever you need in under 5 minutes!

Our Lady of the Oven

This is not a diet book.

It is not a celebrity endorsed weight loss scheme, or an underground cure for cancer. It will not tell you how to eat 30 super foods a day, operate a juicer, avoid carbs, go raw, get ripped, do all your domestic chores in 30 minutes or less, look 20 years younger, save your soul or recycle. If if these are what you're after, I'm afraid you're holding the wrong book.

But if what you're seeking is bliss, all of the light, hearty, sweet, salty, crunchy, soft, soul satisfying, joygasmic food-bliss that most true GF'ers trudge through life lamenting, then welcome. I wrote this book for you. I am one of you.

I was diagnosed with Celiac Disease on my 29th Birthday. At that moment I was actually *thrilled*. To finally know what was wrong with me most of my life, and better yet to know it was something I could control myself, unmedicated, was an immense relief. I bought a few books, some extra fruits and veg and jumped straight into my new gluten free (GF) life.

Two days later, my son turned six. Optimistically I skipped into the store, picked up a gluten free brownie mix, and whipped it up for the party... By the end of said party I was sniffing back big, hot tears of mommy failure. That brownie thing was vile.

The brownie mix was the beginning of the end of my optimism. I tasted and tested, bought and baked, read reviews, then wondered why I'd bothered with the reviews (were they crazy?), for everything GF I could possibly get my hands on. "Surely it can't all be that bad," slowly devolved into, "It's not. Some of it is way worse," and then finally, "OMFG, did I just get really excited because that wasn't revolting?!" It only took four months for what I had seen as a blessing to metamorphose into a full curse. Celiac, as most of you know, is genetic. My tiny, frail, toddler daughter was soon diagnosed with Celiac Disease just like mommy, and then my son with gluten intolerance. Both of my children were sick and I couldn't even provide good food for them. I slid straight down the guilt slide and splashed into a pool of depression, only occasionally lightened by comically long rants about cardboard and sand and how those things need to be on the label if companies were going to keep making bread out of them. But I had passed my dented genes onto two innocent children, and in effect destroyed food-normal for them forever. That guilt boulder was massive.

Fast forward to my son's 7th birthday. I was terrified of even the expectation of cake, so ever the logical woman that I am, I pretended it didn't exist. Cake? What cake? My strategy was remarkably effective, too, until about 2 hours before the party when the boy gleefully declared, "I want a vanilla cake!" I stumbled to the kitchen in a daze, set two bowls onto the counter and watched as a minute spark of divine inspiration ignited a massive pocket of highly compressed maniacal desperation and exploded. When the dust cleared and the oven timer beeped, I beheld my first miracle; vanilla cupcakes. I had made real, tender, moist vanilla cupcakes and they were *good*. The clouds in my mind parted like the Red Sea. If one amazing gluten free food was possible, so were more. They had to be. There was a mountain before me and I had to climb it, to conquer it, to look out from the summit and see the world altered, my guilt boulder a tiny pebble.

As I descend now from my sacred mission, commandments in hand, the taste of the divine still upon my lips, I overflow with gratitude, not for talent or a divine gift, but for my children. My sweet, silly, obnoxious, amazing, celiac children. Only for their sakes could I summon the strength to steal back these rays of sunshine from that rotten jailor, disease. Only in working to save their pleasures was I able to rediscover my own.

Little, stolen scraps of bliss. That's what this book is.

Herein you will find the food I believe worthy of my children's memories. I present it to you in hopes that perhaps you too might find a little of what you need, what you miss, in it. Salvation of the unadulterated love of food, mine and yours, this is my Holy Grail. Drink deeply.

Seven Most Divine and Holy Commandments of Gluten Free Baking

1

Thou shalt not taint your baked goods with the insidious rice flour

Rice flour has no flavor. It is devoid of nutrition. But worst of all evils, it changes otherwise delectable baked goods into grainy, sandy, gummy, brittle, empty carb nuggets of nastiness that only the truly desperate could imagine themselves enjoying. Leave the rice to be served with curry or wrapped in sushi where its virtues may shine through; it does not belong in your cookies.

2

Thou shalt not ingest the bitter tapioca starch

Tapioca flour burns at a low temperature, that's why so many GF recipes use it to help their rice flour abominations "brown." Burnt tapioca flour tastes bitter at best, and the unpleasantness of the flavor lingers creating an unholy aftertaste that will send the sane running for their tooth brushes. Reject this evil.

3

Thou shalt not demand an all-purpose flour mix

Do we use all-purpose house keys? One prescription fits all eye glasses? No, because they would no longer serve their purpose. The same is true of the dry ingredients in a recipe. Unless you want cupcakes with the texture of biscotti you need to use the appropriate tool for the job, and that means changing the type and amount of flour accordingly. Even a good gluten baker knows there are important times to use cake flour vs. white vs. whole wheat vs. starch. It is ridiculous to imagine that truly enjoyable gluten free (GF) baking should be simpler than its traditional counterpart. You cannot attain gluten free nirvana if you refuse to honor the extra few moments it takes to get there.

4

Thou shalt not make random substitutions on the first try

Generally, It. Won't. Work. Particularly with flours (see commandment 3). Even if you are exceptionally confident in your own baking substitution skills, you cannot know whether your changes have improved, or practically destroyed, a recipe if you do not first bake the thing exactly as it is written. Good experiments demand a control. Have faith. Bake it as written the first time. After that, have fun! Experiment all you like with my full blessings. (This obviously does not apply to necessary substitutions due to food allergies and intolerances. See the allergen chart on pages 102-105 for assistance.)

5

Thou shalt verify the Gluten Free (GF) status of every single ingredient

The supreme evil one (gluten) sneaks into everything, in fields, in storage facilities, on packaging equipment; you cannot know if an item is gluten free by merely examining the ingredients. Obviously, this is mainly a problem for those of us with Celiac disease or severe allergies, so if that's not you, feel free to skip it by. But if your condition can be affected by small amounts of gluten (which includes everyone with Celiac Disease), you need to be wary. The US has only recently adopted a legal definition for the term "gluten free," which won't be enforced until mid 2014. That means that any company looking to tap into a new market can still slap those words on their product without fear of legal action against them. What does that mean? Basically, you could scribble "gluten free" on a bag of wheat flour and still sell it with out punishment in the US, at least until mid 2014. Scary, huh? The situation will improve when labeling laws become enforceable, but even then foods are only required to test below 20 parts per million with no regard for how that's managed or whether known low-level contamination exists. Low-level contamination does affect many Celiacs though, and in my opinion the definition even once enforceable will be too lax to be really helpful.

Instead, look for third party, gluten free certification; certification is your surest bet that a product is truly GF. And be ready to call the manufacturer of anything that's not certified to ask specifically about the possibility of contamination. I have not labeled any of the ingredients in my recipes as "gluten free" because to be safe you must verify that ALL ingredients are GF, not just a few problem ones. Do not condemn this author for not reminding you on every page to choose GF oat flour, GF xanthan gum, etc. It's just redundant. But please, please, please do care for yourself by thoroughly checking your ingredients and not contaminating yourself in your own home. Symptoms that come with minuscule contamination may not be acute or severe in all Celiacs, but repeated contamination will affect your recovery.

6

Thou shalt not bake without an accurate oven thermometer

Buy one. They are cheap, and ovens, even brand new ones, can be wildly inaccurate. Do not subject yourself to the agonies of mysteriously burnt cookies or breads with doughy, mushy middles. Shield yourself and your family from the myriad woes of scorched cupcakes! Always use a thermometer, place it near the center of the oven where your food will be, and adjust the heat accordingly.

7

Thou shalt honor the awesomeness of the Holy Digital Kitchen Scale

Weighing your ingredients is more accurate, and with practice, faster and easier than messing about with multiple, messy, measuring cups. Choose a scale that can switch between ounces and grams (or in a pinch, is purely metric as most recipes written by weight are written in metric), has a tare or zero feature, and has a reputation for being accurate. This one, modest purchase can reduce your prep and clean up time and simultaneously dramatically improve your baking results and consistency. Feel the power!

Know Thy Food

Good food can only be made from good ingredients. Period. This quick guide will help you to understand, find and store everything you need. My sources are mainly US internet sources, sorry rest of the world! **Remember; every type of food can be contaminated with gluten in packaging and handling processes. Please make sure that ALL of your ingredients are truly gluten free!** Look for items that are certified GF, call manufacturers to ask about contamination, and keep yourself safe.

Almond Flour: Finely ground, blanched almonds add retained moisture and a buttery flavor to baked goods as well as protein, healthy fats, lots of minerals, and vitamin E. The oils can cause clumping in the sifter so you'll need the help of a hand or the back of a spoon to rub against the mesh and help break up the clumping. *Never skip sifting almond flour* and choose the finest ground variety available; this is absolutely necessary for good texture.

✔ Store chilled in an airtight container as the fats can spoil. Extra quantities should be frozen for freshness; thaw frozen almond flour on the counter for about an hour before trying to sift it for a recipe.

❤ Nuts.com has, hands down, the best almond flour I've found. Give it a try!

Almond Milk: An excellent replacement for milk in baking. Choose unsweetened varieties that aren't too thick or viscous, or make your own! Soak 1 C raw almonds in plenty of water overnight, then drain, rinse, and blend with 4 C pure water until milky and richly white. Strain through a cheese cloth that has been folded a few times to make it more fine, and it's ready to use. If allergic, you may substitute unsweetened flax, soy or hemp milk.

✔ Store chilled. Homemade lasts about 2-4 days, store brands 7 or more.

❤ Silk Pure Almond is widely available in the US including through amazon.com.

Amaranth Flour: An ancient grain with a light flavor, reminiscent of corn, amaranth offers lots of iron, magnesium, phosphorous, manganese and is a complete protein. It doesn't absorb much moisture though, so it needs to be blended with a starch when baking. Amaranth baked goods also often need to be stored chilled.

✔ Store in an airtight container. It is fairly shelf stable at room temperature except in very warm climates, where it should be stored chilled.

❤ Nuts.com or bobsredmill.com; Bob's Red Mill is also widely available in the US.

Arrowroot Starch: AKA arrowroot powder, this is the starch extracted from the root of the arrowroot plant. It absorbs and retains moisture well, adds lightness and contributes to the overall cohesiveness of baked goods. Unlike most starches, which are nutritionally void, arrowroot is high in calcium and manganese.

✔ Store at room temperature in an airtight container.

❤ Nuts.com or bobsredmill.com; Bob's Red Mill is also widely available in the US.

Baking Powder vs Baking Soda: These are leavening agents, the ingredients that make foods rise or puff up. They do this by releasing gasses when in contact with moisture, acids and/or heat. The difference is that baking soda needs an acidic ingredient in the recipe to react with or it generally will not release enough gas to be effective, whereas baking powder is essentially baking soda premixed with an acid to react to and some starch to pull moisture away from it, therefore it does not depend upon acid ingredients. Some baking powders also contain aluminum, which is something to watch out for to avoid. In a pinch (or if you are corn free) you can make your own baking powder by mixing well **1 part Baking Soda**, **1 part Arrowroot Starch** and **2 parts Cream of Tartar**.

✔ Store in an airtight container at room temperature. Baking soda should be replaced every 3-6 months, store bought baking powder every 6-12, depending on humidity. Both loose their leavening power to moisture in the air.

❤ Bob's Red Mill's Aluminum Free Baking Powder is great and widely available in the US or at bobsredmill.com.

Buckwheat Flour: Not actually wheat, buckwheat is related to sorrel and rhubarb. The flavor is nutty and earthy-sweet like its beautiful dark color. It's also a nutritional powerhouse full of manganese, tryptophan, magnesium, copper and insoluble fiber. That fiber requires special handling though; never skip the lemon juice or resting periods in a buckwheat recipe. Skip and it will come out gritty, but follow the directions and fibers will break down a little, hold moisture, create bonds and give you surprisingly airy, tender results.

✔ Store in an airtight container at room temperature, or in summer/warm climates, store chilled.

❤ Arrowhead Mills is available in many US stores or to the 48 contiguous through arrowheadmills.elsstore.com.

Chocolate Chips: Use regular, mini, chunks, or whatever you can find that you like and is safe for you to eat. Personally I love working with mini chips because they distribute flavor more evenly in cookies and also melt faster for use in other recipes.

✔ Store at room temperature, out of the sun and away from heat sources.

❤ Enjoy Life makes great, safe mini-chips or chunks. Buy locally or from amazon.com or glutenfreemall.com.

Natural Cocoa Powder: This is purely the prepared, ground cocoa bean, pressed to release cocoa butter, then reground to make a fine powder. *Do not use Dutched or Dutch processed cocoa or cocoa processed with alkali for the recipes in this book*, it is a more heavily processed food with less flavor and most importantly, less acidity. Natural cocoa powder is an acid food used to react with baking soda to create leavening, so changing types will result in foods that don't rise properly. Beware of adding more or less cocoa powder for this reason and because cocoa acts as a starch in recipes as well, and therefore its volume is at least as important as that of the other flours.

✔ Store at room temperature, away from direct sunlight.

❤ Rapunzel brand has higher cocoa butter content than most, leaving foods richer and flavors smoother. It really is worth the trouble of seeking out. Available on amazon.com and from loads of other online retailers.

Coconut Milk: High in lauric acid, rich and creamy, coconut milk helps give back some of the richness usually derived from dairy. But not all coconut milk is created equal. When using canned, look for brands with the least extra junk in them that you can find. The additives adversely effect both flavor and texture, usually yielding a gummy, unnaturally viscous product that won't bake up as well. My favorite brand contains only coconut, water, and guar gum. If your kitchen is cooler than about 76°F/24.5°C, then the oil in the milk will solidify. You can remedy this by mixing in a blender, or tossing an unopened can into a bowl of hot tap water and letting it rest until warm, then shaking the can well before opening.

✔ Canned varieties are shelf stable, but must be refrigerated once opened and usually won't last more than a week in the fridge.

❤ Native Forest is my favorite and simply amazing, buy it on amazon.com or directly from edwardandsons.com.

Coconut Palm Sugar: Not to be confused with just "palm sugar," which is a different product, coconut palm sugar is basically the boiled down nectar from coconut palm flowers. It is minimally processed, low on the glycemic index, and has this neat, syrupy flavor that really compliments savory dishes without any overpowering sweetness.

✔ Store in an airtight container at room temperature.

❤ Wholesome Sweeteners' is easy to work with, easy to find, and socially responsible: wholesomesweeteners.com.

Dark Brown Sugar: All types of brown sugar are really just white sugar with some portion of the molasses mixed back in, and dark brown gets more back than most. We use it for its double whammy of rich flavor and increased mineral content to help offset the unhealthy demands of white sugar on the body. You can make your own by adding about ¼ C (86g) of molasses per pound of sugar and mixing very thoroughly in a mixer of food processor.

✔ Store in an airtight container at room temperature. If it hardens to a block, it's simply dried out. Put the dried out sugar in a large bowl and cover the bowl with a damp towel over night (not touching the sugar) and it should look right in the morning.

❤ Wholesome Sweeteners' is rich and moist. Available on amazon.com and wholesomesweeteners.com.

Desiccated Coconut: Also sold as shredded coconut, desiccated coconut is simply pure coconut meat that has been shredded and dried. It is not to be confused with angel flake or any other sweetened variety. The only ingredient should be coconut. It adds flavor, fiber, trace amounts of good fats and a little island flair to baked goods, while contributing to cohesion and texture by retaining moisture.

✔ Store chilled or frozen in an airtight container for best shelf life, particularly in warm climates.

❤ Nuts.com sells theirs as Shredded Coconut; it is certified GF and always excellent. Let's Do… Organic also sells a good GF shredded coconut, edwardandsons.com. Beware: Bob's Red Mill's is *not* GF.

Ground Flax: Also called flax meal, ground flax is full of omega 3s and antioxidants. Most important for us though, flax's amazing proportion of water soluble fiber acts as a binder that also increases viscosity in dough and moisture retention in baked goods, partially replacing the effects of gluten. Golden and brown varieties may be used interchangeably, though the golden is better camouflaged in baked goods if that makes a difference to you.

✔ Store chilled in an airtight container. Fats in ground flax go rancid quickly at room temperature. May be frozen.

♥ Bob's Red Mill's is great, usually inexpensive, and easy to find in US stores, at bobsredmill.com, or amazon.com.

Lemon Juice: In most of my recipes lemon juice is added as an acid to react with baking soda to create rise, or to help break down fibrous flours creating a more tender texture. For this purpose bottled lemon juice is great, perhaps even preferable, as it is generally of a more uniform acidity than fresh. If squeezing fresh, strain and discard the pulp.

✔ Store chilled after opening/squeezing.

♥ Lakewood Organic's is brilliant and very widely available in the US, and on amazon.com.

Maple Syrup: Not to be confused with maple flavored pancake goop, this glittering amber liquid is simply the spring sap of the maple tree, heated to evaporate much of the water. The real thing is sweeter than sugar, delicately and delightfully flavored, and even confers health benefits. I like to use a light grade for the more delicate taste.

✔ Store chilled after opening.

♥ Many good brands are GF and widely available. I like Anderson's and Spring Tree, but I don't have a favorite.

Millet Flour: Millet is an ancient grain with a sweet, subtle flavor that is high in fiber, iron, B vitamins, magnesium and potassium. Its flour lends nutrition and superb flavor to our recipes, but like most GF whole flours, needs the balance of a starch for moisture and texture.

✔ Store chilled, in an airtight container, as the lovely flavor can deteriorate within days if left at room temperature.

♥ Arrowhead Mills' is the best GF millet around. Find at amazon.com or arrowheadmills.elsstore.com.

Oats and Oat Flour: Now we finally have dedicated farmers growing oats far from any wheat fields that are certified GF and absolutely delicious! Hurray! Thank heavens too, because oat flour has a flavor and texture when baked that will delight you. **Do make sure that the oats and oat flour you choose are tested/certified and specifically grown to be gluten free.** Oats grown conventionally are frequently contaminated with gluten straight from the fields and some varieties can be more upsetting to the celiac stomach than others, so caution is imperative. Also be sure to use quick oats rather than rolled oats when called for, as it may significantly alter results.

✔ Store in an airtight container in a cool place. In warm to hot climates, store chilled.

♥ Bob's Red Mill has a complete line of great GF oat products; bobsredmill.com, amazon.com.

Oils: No, one oil is not the same as any other, and yes, your choice matters. Most of my recipes call for grapeseed oil because it remains stable at baking temperatures and has a lovely, fairly neutral flavor profile that works well in baked goods. Can't find it? The best substitute is safflower oil which, in my experience performs, equally well. But take note - they have different densities, so you may need to adjust the weights for the recipe if changing oils. See chart on page 101. Olive oil is also very heat tolerant but has a distinctive flavor, so it's used only in recipes where the flavor is an asset. "Vegetable oil" is generally a mix of genetically modified soy, canola and whatever's cheap that season. It is less heat stable and canola oil has a knack for breaking down and imparting an off, fishy flavor when you least want it too. Those mixes are bad for health, bad for the environment, and lousy in foods. Avoid them, and for taste, avoid even pure canola, particularly in higher heat applications such as in stove top recipes.

✔ Store at room temperature, away from heat or direct sunlight. I stick pour spouts on the bottles for ease of use.

❤ Napa Valley Naturals is my beloved, go-to brand. Find at napavalleynaturals.com or amazon.com.

Palm Oil Shortening: Sure, you could use any kind, but Crisco and the like are a nasty bit of unhealthy, genetically modified, processed, yuck. I use pure palm oil, which is not hydrogenated, has the perfect firmness at room temperature, is flavor neutral and heat stable. Great stuff! Please note: if you do choose to use the main stream hydrogenated stuff, you will have to adjust the weights in the recipe. The hydrogenated goop is more dense than the unaltered palm oil that I recommend. See chart on page 101.

✔ Store at room temperature, very shelf stable.

❤ Spectrum Naturals' is perfect! Find it at spectrumorganics.com, amazon.com, and loads of other stores & sites. NOTE: To my knowledge this is the only gluten free Spectrum product because it is made in a separate plant; their other oils are pressed on the same equipment as their wheat germ oil, so I avoid everything else from this company.

Potato Starch: Not to be confused with the very potato-y potato flour, potato starch is dense, silky, and flavorless. I use it sparingly, because it adds nothing nutritionally to a recipe, but it does offer unique and, at times indispensable, silky, moist texture which is exquisite in the right recipe.

✔ Store at room temperature, extremely shelf stable.

❤ Bob's Red Mill's is reliably great. Find in stores or at bobsredmill.com or amazon.com.

Powdered Sugar: Thanks to its extra fine grind and the small amount of corn starch in it, powdered sugar can thicken, retain moisture, create a finer crumb, and sweeten all at once. For those avoiding corn, Wholesome Sweeteners sells a corn free variety, but it tends to need more sifting than most. Sifting is crucial for powdered sugar as any moisture in the air can create clumping which even on a small scale will alter the taste and texture of baked goods and frostings unfavorably.

✔ Store at room temperature in an airtight container and away from moisture.

❤ Any GF brand will do, and they are widely available: wholesomesweeteners.com or amazon.com.

Quinoa Flour: Quinoa flour is high in protein, incredibly nutrient dense, and a valuable asset for texture. It also has a very strong flavor that some love, but others may find disagreeable. It is definitely best tempered with other flours for flavor, and is not over used in this book, in spite of its nutritional value. Certain varieties may also cause reactions in some Celiacs, so if you've had a bad experience with quinoa, you may want to avoid it or try a different brand or type to find a variety that agrees with you and your immune system.

✔ In very cool climates, store at room temperature in an air tight container, but in warm climates, store chilled.

❤ Nuts.com offers a nice, fine flour that's less pungent than most, digests easily. and is definitely my favorite!

Raw Honey: Yes, I know it's expensive, and sorry, but no, you can't just use regular pasteurized honey. To spare you expense, I've tried to only use as little as possible in recipes where it really makes them work. Raw honey does so much for baking that the stuff in the bear simply can't. The live enzymes it carries help to break down some of the intensely fibrous GF flours, tenderizing your baked goods. The thick, sticky texture helps hold foods together better. And raw honey has a light, sweet taste that is not over powering and really shines in breads and muffins. (For the record, the stuff in the bear tastes beyond awful in bread; trust me, I got desperate once...)

✔ Store at room temperature, pretty much indefinitely.

❤ Honey Bunny from Canada is the best around! Well worth going out of your way for: www.honeybunny.ca.

Sorghum Flour: It has the closest flavor profile to wheat flour of all the GF flours I've found, but offers very little nutrition, so it is best used only in minimally flavored dishes where a more nutritious, but also more obtrusively flavorful, flour would be undesirable.

✔ Store at room temperature in an airtight container.

❤ I use Bob's Red Mill, available at bobsredmill.com, amazon.com.

Xanthan Gum: By far the weirdest ingredient in GF baking, Xanthan made from the slimy-gummy stuff produced by a specific bacterium as it feeds on glucose. Despite its awkward origins, his powder does more to replace the binding effects of gluten than any other ingredient, making it possible for us to have fluffy baked goods that don't crumble and fall apart. On its own, it smells like glue, and if too much is used it will impart a bad flavor. Thankfully that's avoidable by using only just enough. Most xanthan producing cultures are fed on glucose from corn, so if you have corn allergies and are very sensitive, you may want to stick to recipes that work without, or with guar gum. *I haven't tested all the recipes here with guar gum, and it is very much not a perfect substitute! But generally, for cupcakes, muffins and rolls, use double the amount of xanthan called for.* **CAUTION:** Bob's Red Mill's xanthan is from cultures fed on wheat starch. It is tested to not contain more than 20ppm gluten, but in my head that makes it a dangerously grey area at best. I personally feel better physically when using other brands.

✔ Store in an airtight container at room temperature; don't leave it open longer than required in humid air.

❤ Hodgson Mills' performs beautifully and comes in small packets. Buy my favorite at www.hodgsonmillstore.com.

Thy Holy Instruments

Whisk: Essential for quickly and easily combining flours and beating together batters in a fraction of the time as with a spoon. Get one. Use it often. Heck, get two. ...I have three.

Silicone Scraper: There are many types and shapes of scrapers out there; the ones I use are the "silicone spatulas" made by Roslë which I highly recommend. Their groovy design doesn't harbor food residues or fall apart. Use them to cream flax into shortening, scrape all of your batter out of the bowl, cut thicker wet ingredients into flour efficiently, loosen baked goods from nonstick pans, and even for sautéing on the stove top. In my opinion, a good scraper is a kitchen essential. (I won't tell you how many of these I have. Trust me, it's better that you not know.)

Sifter: GF flours need sifting. Whether or not you sift will almost always be obvious in the end result, so don't skip the extra minute it takes to turn the crank. There are many different types of sifters out there and I've tried most of them, but nothing works better for the recipes in this book than a simple, cheap, hand cranked-sifter with the arched bars inside that turn. Choose one that has the longest contact area between the mesh and the bars that you can find. More contact means flours push through more quickly and easily. But remember that nut flours will still need a little encouragement from the back of a spoon scraping it through in the end.

Digital Kitchen Scale: In a word, indispensable. See Commandment 7. To use, plop your bowl on top, set your sifter in the bowl if weighing flour, and turn the scale on. Pour in one ingredient until you've got the right amount. Hit the tare or zero button to reset to zero, pour next ingredient in, an so on. It's a huge time and labor saver once you get the hang of it, especially with ingredients like shortening and peanut butter. Your baked goods will also turn out better and show more consistent results because it's so much more precise than using measuring cups.

Loaf, Cake, and Muffin Pans: I'm devoted to stainless steel. It is no fuss, durable, dishwasher safe, conducts heat efficiently, doesn't warp in the oven, releases food beautifully with only a light greasing, and there are no concerns about toxicity as with aluminum and nonstick pans. Even if you aren't willing to jump on the stainless bandwagon, do use metal pans unless specified in the recipe. Substituting earthenware, Corning Ware or glass type bakeware will at best alter cooking times and at worst ruin a recipe. Paying attention to pan type is important. The same goes for specified pan sizes or cakes that call for a bundt/tube pan. Those recipes need the specific level of heat penetration that the pans called for will provide. For GF breads especially, pan size is crucial to the success of the recipe.

Parchment Paper: For me, parchment is non-optional. Easy cake removal, breads that rise and stay higher thanks to un-greased pans, cookies that brown perfectly and never stick, parchment does so much, and with minimal trapping of moisture. You can also save money and resources by reusing your parchment. Wait for it to dry, gently wipe it free of crumbs with a kitchen towel and it's good to go for another round. I reuse the cookie sheet sized pieces until they either rip or wear out. The cake and loaf pan pieces last through 2-6 bakings. I know a lot of people now are using *silicone baking mats* for their reusability. But while the mats are awesome for rolling out dough on (I highly recommend them for this), they aren't good heat conductors and trap moisture during baking so foods don't crisp or brown the way they should. I have two silicone mats, but I refuse to bake with them.

Baking Cups: These are the paper liners used for cupcakes and muffins. Though not crucial kitchen items, they are handy, facilitating both easy sharing and quick cleanup. The best ones I've found are made by If You Care; they are ecological, chlorine free, perfectly sized, and they don't stick to or absorb the oils from your recipe. I love them.

Mixing Bowls: The most important feature of a mixing bowl is its size, though a nice, deep style can also be handy to help prevent slopping batter over the sides. For our purposes, be sure to have an absolute minimum of 2 bowls. One needs to be at least a 5qt/4.5-5 L size, and the second in the 3-5qt/3-5 L range. Unless you will be using a mixer, always use the larger bowl for your dry ingredients because the whole recipe comes together in that bowl.

Cookie Sheets: Not to be confused with a jelly roll pan, which has four short, raised sides in order to contain a very shallow cake batter, a cookie sheet will have a *maximum* of three raised sides, usually opening at a nice wide angle. Why is this important? The raised sides of a jelly roll pan shield the edges of the cookies from the heat in a way that limits proper, even browning. The sides also make it much more difficult to slip a hot, fragile cookie off of the pan without breaking it. A real cookie sheet poses neither problem and with those small differences will give you tastier, easier cookies. I highly recommend having two good cookie sheets so that you can be loading up the next while on is in the oven. This will save you time and energy costs far in excess of the cost of the extra pan.

Rolling Pin: I am truly devoted to my simple, tapered French pin. I've used a wide variety of rolling pins, marble, silicone coated, with handles, a straight dowel, one with spacers, etc. In my experience nothing beats that lovely taper for maneuvering around the edges of a dough that likes to split, which most of our GF ones really love to do.

Stand Mixer: Yes, I own one, and yes, I love it. I do not use it for most recipes though, because it's just not needed for simple batters. Save the heavy equipment for creaming the sugar into the fat for cookies, or fluffing up an awesome frosting. Most recipes in this book can be made quickly and easily with just the aforementioned whisk, scraper and a couple of bowls. If you have a physical reason for not mixing your batters by hand, arthritis for example, you certainly may use a mixer for any recipe in this book, but do beware of over beating. Stick to low settings and very short mixing times to mimic hand mixing unless the recipe specifies otherwise.

Cake Strips: These are basically flexible strips made of silicone, cloth, or some other insulating material that may be wrapped and fastened around the outside of a round, layer cake pan, and left on while baking. Their purpose is to keep the sides of the cakes from crusting too soon and ceasing to rise. Using them gives you a fairly level cake with a better, more even rise without a single recipe change. I have yet to find or make really great strips, so I can't recommend a brand or method, but if you have any interest in baking layer cakes I do recommend trying some. A word of caution: do not use them on any type of pan other than 8 or 9 inch (20-23 cm) layer pans. If the recipe calls for a larger or more specific pan size, then that recipe will need the heat to arrive unobstructed.

Specialty Items: Most pieces of specialty equipment called for here are not expensive, and are needed for one unusual recipe, like muffin rings for making English Muffins, or a waffle iron for waffles (I adamantly recommend one that flips or turns over). If the recipe in question is one you might use often, then it makes good sense to get what is needed to make it most easily. You will struggle less and generally be happier with the results using the right equipment, and therefore will be more likely to keep cooking.

Interpreting the Scriptures

As High Priestess of the Oven, I hereby decree that looking back and forth between ingredient lists and separate instructions gives me an unholy headache. I refuse to perpetuate such unnecessary suffering.

Instructions
are designated by bullets to make it easier to find your place in the recipe. Instructions for handling ingredients generally precede the list of ingredients so you know what you'll be doing with all that stuff on your counter.

Ingredients
are indented and printed in bold so they can be a part of the recipe, but also remain clearly visible for preparing and shopping.

Measurements
Please note that *all cup, tablespoon, and teaspoon measurements are US customary measurements*, which are smaller than those of the same name in most other countries. The Tb and tsp though are close enough to the metric size to use them interchangeably.

Most recipes will call for the use of a **"dry bowl"** and a **"wet bowl."** These should just be medium to large mixing bowls, each designated for this recipe to hold either dry or wet ingredients that need to be premixed. The dry bowl should be large enough to mix the final batter in.

The pan heading here will tell you what type of pan to use for cooking or baking the recipe.

Instructions to preheat oven are often arbitrarily listed immediately under the pan heading. Unless the recipe calls for chilling dough or allowing batter to rest, you will probably want to begin preheating sooner, depending upon how long it usually takes your oven to come to temperature.

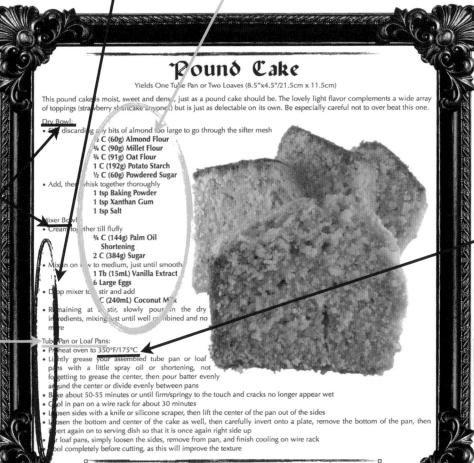

Pound Cake

Yields One Tube Pan or Two Loaves (8.5"x4.5"/21.5cm x 11.5cm)

This pound cake is moist, sweet and dense, just as a pound cake should be. The lovely light flavor complements a wide array of toppings (strawberry shortcake anyone?) but is just as delectable on its own. Be especially careful not to over beat this one.

Dry Bowl:
- Sift, discarding any bits of almond too large to go through the sifter mesh
  - **1 C (60g) Almond Flour**
  - **¾ C (90g) Millet Flour**
  - **¾ C (91g) Oat Flour**
  - **1 C (192g) Potato Starch**
  - **½ C (60g) Powdered Sugar**
- Add, then whisk together thoroughly
  - **1 tsp Baking Powder**
  - **1 tsp Xanthan Gum**
  - **1 tsp Salt**

Mixer Bowl:
- Cream together till fluffy
  - **¾ C (144g) Palm Oil Shortening**
  - **2 C (384g) Sugar**
- Mix on low to medium, just until smooth
  - **1 Tb (15mL) Vanilla Extract**
  - **6 Large Eggs**
- Drop mixer to stir and add
  - **1 C (240mL) Coconut Milk**
- Remaining at a stir, slowly pour in the dry ingredients, mixing just until well combined and no more

Tube Pan or Loaf Pans:
- Preheat oven to 350°F/175°C
- Lightly grease your assembled tube pan or loaf pans with a little spray oil or shortening, not forgetting to grease the center, then pour batter evenly around the center or divide evenly between pans
- Bake about 50-55 minutes or until firm/springy to the touch and cracks no longer appear wet
- Cool in pan on a wire rack for about 30 minutes
- Loosen sides with a knife or silicone scraper, then lift the center of the pan out of the sides
- Loosen the bottom and center of the cake as well, then carefully invert onto a plate, remove the bottom of the pan, then invert again on to serving dish so that it is once again right side up
- For loaf pans, simply loosen the sides, remove from pan, and finish cooling on wire rack
- Cool completely before cutting, as this will improve the texture

Our Daily Breads

Breads

Quick Breads

Rolls & Biscuits

Compliment

Small Sandwich Bread

Yields 4 Small Loaves (5.5"x3"/14 cm x 7.5 cm)

Awesome texture and a lovely, light flavor make for a moist, tender sandwich, just smaller in scale. This recipe doesn't bake well in a large loaf, but is magic in miniature. Little sandwiches are adorable in a lunch box too, just make more! Toasts delectably as well.

Dry Bowl:
- Sift, discarding any bits of almond too large to pass through the sifter mesh
  - **¾ C (90g) Almond Flour**
  - **¾ C (90g) Amaranth Flour**
  - **½ C (64g) Sorghum Flour**
  - **1 C (128g) Arrowroot Starch**
- Add, then whisk together thoroughly
  - **1 ½ tsp Baking Powder**
  - **1 tsp Baking Soda**
  - **1 tsp Xanthan Gum**
  - **½ tsp Salt**

Wet Bowl:
- Beat together until mostly uniform in color
  - **2 Tb (13g) Ground Flax**
  - **2 Tb (27g) Grapeseed Oil**
  - **3 Tb (62g) Raw Honey**
  - **1 Tb (15mL) Lemon Juice**
  - **3 Large Eggs**
- Whisk in gently
  - **1 ¼ C (300mL) Water**

Mini Loaf Pans:
- Preheat oven to 350°F/175°C
- Grease the bottoms of the pans well with spray oil or shortening
- Pour the wet ingredients into the dry and whisk together just until a smooth batter forms
- Pour batter evenly into the 4 pans; they should only be around half-full
- Bake for 30 minutes, or until well risen and firm to the touch, with cracks no longer appearing wet
- Cool in pan for 10 minutes only, then loosen the sides with a knife or scraper
- Remove from pan to a wire rack to cool
- Do not slice until completely cooled
- Store in a sealed container or ziplock bag with a paper towel inside to absorb excess moisture

Whole Grain Bread with Oats

Yields 4 Small Loaves (5.5"x3"/14 cm x 7.5 cm)

I've always been a whole grain sort of girl, and a toast sort of girl, and well, allow the two to converge and let's just say you'd definitely have my attention. Whole grain toast was probably the single most relied upon comfort food of my pre-diagnosis life. Losing it left a gaping hole in my heart and on my palate, until this darling recipe finally filled the void. I rely upon it, I relish it, and I toast it up for myself and my kids every chance I get. One word of caution, when very fresh, the honey can stick a little in the toaster oven, so expect that the day it's made.

Dry Bowl:
- Sift, discarding any bits of almond too large to go through the sifter mesh

> **¾ C (90g) Almond Flour**
> **⅔ C (80g) Amaranth Flour**
> **1 C (128g) Arrowroot Starch**
> **⅓ C (40g) Oat Flour**
> **⅓ C (37g) Quinoa Flour**

- Add, then whisk together to thoroughly combine

> **2 tsp Baking Powder**
> **1 tsp Baking Soda**
> **1 ½ tsp Xanthan Gum**
> **½ tsp Salt**

Wet Bowl:
- Whisk together, gently at first, until the honey is completely mixed in

> **3 Tb (20g) Ground Flax**
> **2 Tb (27g) Grapeseed Oil**
> **3 Tb (62g) Raw Honey**
> **3 LargeEggs**
> **1 Tb (15mL) Lemon Juice**

- Gently whisk in

> **1 ⅔ C (400mL) Unsweetened Almond Milk**

Small Loaf Pans:
- Preheat oven to 350°F/175°C
- Lightly grease your mini loaf pans with spray oil or shortening
- Pour wet ingredients over dry and whisk together just until well mixed, then fold in

> **⅔ C (64g) Quick Cook Oats**

- Pour the batter into the pans, dividing it evenly between them; they should only be a little more than ½ full
- Bake for 32-34 minutes or until well risen, nicely browned, firm, and the cracks no longer appear wet
- Cool in pan for 10 minutes only, then loosen sides with a knife or scraper
- Remove from pan to a wire rack to cool; do not slice until completely cooled
- Store in a sealed container or ziplock bag with a paper towel inside to absorb excess moisture

Oat Bread

Yields 1 Large Loaf (8.5"x4.5"/21.5 cm x 11.5 cm) or 3-4 Small Loaves (5.5"x3"/14 cm x 7.5 cm)

This bread has lightly oaty, slightly sweet, whole grain flavor, crust that doesn't go too dark, and brilliant texture. Lovely for sandwiches, and extra bits are perfect in salmon cakes or burgers.

Dry Bowl:
- Sift, discarding any chunks of oat or almond too large to go through the sifter mesh
    - **1 C (120g) Almond Flour**
    - **1 C (121g) Oat Flour**
    - **1 C (128g) Arrowroot Starch**
- Add, then whisk together thoroughly
    - **1 tsp Baking Powder**
    - **1 tsp Baking Soda**
    - **1 tsp Xanthan**
    - **½ tsp Salt**

Wet Bowl:
- Beat together until roughly uniform in color
    - **⅓ C (35g) Ground Flax**
    - **¼ C (79g) Maple Syrup**
    - **2 Tb (27g) Grapeseed Oil**
    - **2 Large Eggs**
- Whisk in gently
    - **1 Tb (15mL) Lemon Juice**
    - **1 ¼ C (300mL) Unsweetened Almond Milk**

Loaf Pan(s):
- Preheat oven to 350°F/175°C
- For large loaves, cut a strip of parchment as wide as the bottom width of your loaf pan and lay it inside covering only the bottom and ends of the pan
- For small loaves, grease only the bottoms of the pans with spray oil or shortening
- Pour the wet ingredients into the dry and whisk together just until a smooth batter forms
- Pour batter evenly into the ungreased pan and smooth the top, or divide evenly between the smaller, greased pans
- Bake small loaves for about 38 minutes, large loaves for 1 hour, or until well risen, browned and the deepest cracks in the crust no longer appear wet or doughy
- Cool in pan 20-30 min for large, 5-10 min for small, then loosen the sides, remove any parchment, and cool on a wire rack
- Do not slice or store until completely cooled
- Store in a sealed container or ziplock type bag with a paper towel inside to absorb excess moisture
- Refrigeration is recommended after the first day, particularly in very hot climates

Buckwheat Bread

Yields 1 Large Loaf (8.5"x4.5"/21.5 cm x 11.5 cm) or 4 Small Loaves (5.5"x3"/14 cm x 7.5 cm)

This earthy, dark bread is springy, moist and a little sweet with a blissfully crispy crust when toasted. Try adding a cup of chopped nuts to make a hearty, heavenly toast for your morning meal.

Dry Bowl:
- Sift, discarding any chunks of almond too large to go through the sifter mesh
  - **1 ½ C (180g) Buckwheat Flour**
  - **½ C (60g) Almond Flour**
  - **1 C (128g) Arrowroot Starch**
- Add, then whisk together to thoroughly combine
  - **1 ½ tsp Baking Powder**
  - **1 tsp Baking Soda**
  - **1 tsp Xanthan Gum**
  - **1 tsp Salt**

Wet Bowl:
- Whisk together just until well mixed
  - **⅓ C (35g) Ground Flax**
  - **3 Tb (40g) Grapeseed Oil**
  - **¼ C (79g) Maple Syrup**
  - **1 Tb (15mL) Lemon Juice**
  - **2 Large Eggs**
- Stir in gently
  - **1 ½ C (350mL) Water**

Loaf Pan(s):
- Preheat oven to 350°F/175°C
- For large loaves, cut a strip of parchment as wide as the bottom width of your loaf pan and lay it inside covering only the bottom and ends of pan
- For small loaves, grease only the bottoms of your pans with spray oil or shortening
- Pour the wet ingredients into the dry and whisk together just until a smooth batter forms
- Pour batter evenly into the ungreased pan and smooth the top, or divide evenly between the smaller, greased pans
- Bake small loaves for 36 minutes, regular loaves for about 1 hour, or until well risen, browned and the deepest cracks in the crust no longer appear wet or doughy
- Cool in pan 20-30 min for large, 5-10 min for small, then loosen the sides, remove any parchment, and cool on a wire rack
- Do not slice or store until completely cooled
- Store in a sealed container or ziplock type bag with a paper towel inside to absorb excess moisture
- Refrigeration is recommended after the first day or two, particularly in very hot climates

Herbed Bread

Yields 1 Large Loaf (8.5"x4.5"/21.5 cm x 11.5 cm) or 4 Small Loaves (5.5"x3"/14 cm x 7.5 cm) or 24 Rolls

Wonderfully aromatic and savory, heady with the scent of rosemary, this is excellent bread for buttering and eating with a bowl of soup or stew, grilling up into truly lovely grilled sandwiches, or even crumbling up leftovers for a flavorful stuffing.

Dry Bowl:
- Sift, discarding any bits of oat or almond too large to go through the sifter mesh

  ½ C (61g) Oat Flour
  ½ C (60g) Almond Flour
  ½ C (60g) Millet Flour
  ½ C (64g) Sorghum Flour
  1 C (128g) Arrowroot Starch
- Add, then whisk together to thoroughly combine

  1 ½ tsp Baking Powder
  1 tsp Baking Soda
  1 tsp Salt
  1 ½ tsp Xanthan Gum

Wet Bowl:
- Beat together until well mixed

  ⅓ C (35g) Ground Flax
  2 Tb (24g) Coconut Palm Sugar
  3 Tb (41g) Olive Oil
  1 Tb (15mL) Lemon Juice
  2 Large Eggs
  2 Tb Fresh Rosemary, chopped
  2 Tb Fresh Sage, chopped
  1 Tb Fresh Parsley, chopped
  1 tsp Fresh Dill, chopped
  1 tsp Dried Coriander
  ½ tsp Onion Powder
- Gently whisk in

  1 ½ C (350mL) Water

Loaf Pan(s) or Muffin Tins:
- Preheat oven to 350°F/175°C
- For large loaves, cut a strip of parchment as wide as the bottom of your loaf pan and lay it in so that it covers only the bottom and ends of pan; for mini loaves, grease only the bottom of the pans, for rolls grease the muffin tins well
- Pour the wet ingredients into the dry and whisk together just until a smooth batter forms
- Pour batter evenly into pan(s), smoothing top gently; for rolls, just spoon into the tins
- Bake regular loaf for 1 hour, mini loaves and rolls for 30-32 min, or until cracks no longer appear wet and loaf feels firm
- Cool in the pan for 20 minutes, 10 for mini loaves, 2 for rolls, then run a knife or scraper around the edges of pan to loosen
- Remove from pans, remove parchment if used, and cool completely on wire rack; do not slice until completely cool

Cinnamon Raisin Bread

Yields 1 Large Loaf (8.5"x4.5"/21.5 cm x 11.5 cm)

Moist, sweet and flavorful, this bread is absolutely great all on its own, and just as good slathered with "butter," toasted, or joy of joys, whipped up into French toast! One note: this recipe requires a long rest period.

Small Bowl:
- Cover with water and allow to soak
        ½ C (83g) Raisins or Currents

Dry Bowl:
- Sift, discarding any bits of almond too large to go through the sifter mesh
        1 C (120g) Almond Flour
        ½ C (60g) Amaranth Flour
        ½ C (64g) Arrowroot Starch
        ½ C (96g) Potato Starch
- Add, then whisk all together to thoroughly combine
        1 Tb Baking Powder
        1 ½ tsp Xanthan Gum
        ½ tsp Salt
        1 Heaping Tb Cinnamon
        ¼ tsp Clove

Wet Bowl:
- Beat together gently at first, until the honey is completely mixed in
        ½ C (165g) Raw Honey
        ¼ C (54g) Grapeseed Oil
        3 Large Eggs
- Whisk in gently
        1 C (240mL) Unsweetened Almond Milk

Loaf Pan:
- Cut a strip of parchment as wide as the bottom of your loaf pan and lay it in so that it only covers the bottom and ends of the pan
- Pour the contents of the wet bowl into the dry and whisk together into a smooth batter
- Drain the raisins and using a silicone scraper or large spoon, fold into the batter with
        ½ C (59g) Chopped Raw Walnuts
- Pour batter evenly into the ungreased pan and smooth the top; cover with plastic wrap and chill for 6 hours or overnight
- Preheat oven to 350°F/175°C; while it heats, let your loaf rest on the counter to warm a little
- Bake for about 1 hour, or until cracks appear mostly dry; if your oven has an upper heating element, you may need to lay a piece of foil gently over the top of the loaf half way through to prevent over-browning
- Cool for 30 minutes in the pan on a wire rack, then loosen the sides, lift out the loaf and peel of the parchment
- Cool on a wire rack to room temperature before slicing
- Store chilled after the first day

Gingerbread

Yields One 14"x9"/35.5 cm x 23 cm Pan of Bread

This bread is light, tender, nicely crumbed and rich with nutrients, minerals and health protecting spices. The flavor improves in the day or two after baking, so it's ideal for gifting or for picking at yourself. A square of this gingerbread and a small cup of vanilla almond milk are one of my absolute favorite snacks year round.

Dry Bowl:
- Sift, discarding any bits of almond or oat too large to go through the sifter mesh

    ½ C (60g) Almond Flour
    1 C (128g) Arrowroot Starch
    1 C (120g) Buckwheat Four
    ½ C (61g) Oat Flour

- Add, then whisk all together thoroughly

    ¼ C (26g) Ground Flax
    1 ½ tsp Baking Soda
    ½ tsp Baking Powder
    1 tsp Xanthan Gum
    1 ½ tsp Ginger
    2 tsp Cinnamon
    ¼ tsp Clove
    ¼ tsp Coriander
    ¼ tsp Cardamom
    ¼ tsp Nutmeg

Wet Bowl:
- Cream together with a silicone scraper or similar

    ½ C (96g) Palm Oil Shortening
    ½ C (96g) Sugar

- Whisk in until thoroughly combined

    2 Large Eggs
    1 C (345g) Molasses

- Gently whisk in

    ¾ C (175mL) Water

14x9 Non-metal Baking Pan:
- Preheat oven to 325°F/160°C
- Grease the bottom of your pan with a little spray oil or shortening
- Pour the wet ingredients into the dry and beat together until a smooth batter forms
- Pour batter into the pan and level it with your spoon or scraper
- Bake for about 34 minutes or until it appears set and the top is cracking
- Cool in the pan on a wire rack for at least 20 minutes before slicing into squares
- Cool completely before storing in an airtight container, I just use plastic wrap or a lid atop the pan it baked in

Banana Bread

Yields 4 Small Loaves (5.5"x3"/14 cm x 7.5 cm) or 1 Tube Pan

Tender and sweet but hearty with whole grains, banana bread was always a special treat when I was growing up. My grandmother would bake some up anytime we had too many bananas, keep one loaf out and freeze the rest, saving it for the summer when she would be loath to turn on the oven. I still remember the addictive, moist-sweet taste of it cold from the fridge on a warm afternoon. Try it! This recipe freezes superbly.

Dry Bowl:
- Sift, discarding any bits of almond or oat too large to go through the sifter mesh
  - **1 C (120g) Millet Flour**
  - **½ C (61g) Oat Flour**
  - **½ C (60g) Almond Flour**
  - **½ C (96g) Potato Starch**
- Add, then whisk all together thoroughly
  - **1 tsp Xanthan Gum**
  - **1 tsp Salt**
  - **1 tsp Baking Powder**
  - **1 tsp Baking Soda**

Wet Bowl:
- Whisk together vigorously until mostly uniform in color
  - **1 C (200g) Dark Brown Sugar, not packed**
  - **3 Tb (40g) Grapeseed Oil**
  - **3 Large Eggs**
  - **2 ⅔ C (630mL) Puréed Banana**

Tube Pan or Loaf Pans:
- Preheat the oven to 325°F/160°C

- Lightly grease pan of choice with spray oil or shortening
- Pour the wet ingredients into the dry and beat together until a smooth batter forms
- Pour batter evenly into pan(s) gently smoothing the tops
- Bake 40 minutes for tube pans, 35 min for small loaves, or until it springs back when pressed lightly in the center
- For small loaves, cool in pan for 5 minutes, then loosen sides, remove from pan and allow to cool on a wire rack
- For tube pans, cool 10 minutes in the pan, then loosen the sides and around the center, if your pan is two pieces also lift it free of the sides and loosen the bottom of the bread, now gently invert onto a plate, lift the pan free and re-invert onto a serving plate or wire rack
- Cool completely before storing in an airtight container

Sweet Dinner Rolls
Yields 18 Rolls

Golden, sweet and savory, moist and light, these rolls are certain to delight. Serve with soup, spread with "butter" or just eat them out of hand. They're especially divine still warm from the oven!

Dry Bowl:
- Sift, discarding any bits of almond too large to go through the sifter mesh
  - **¾ C (90g) Almond Flour**
  - **½ C (60g) Millet Flour**
  - **¼ C (30g) Amaranth Flour**
  - **½ C (64g) Arrowroot Starch**
  - **½ C (96g) Potato Starch**
- Add, then whisk all together thoroughly
  - **1 Tb Baking Powder**
  - **1 ½ tsp Xanthan Gum**
  - **½ tsp Salt**

Wet Bowl:
- Whisk together until it becomes roughly uniform in color
  - **½ C (100g) Dark Brown Sugar, not packed**
  - **½ C (108g) Grapeseed Oil**
  - **3 Large Eggs**
- Add and whisk in thoroughly
  - **1 C plus 2 Tb (270mL) Unsweetened Almond Milk**

Muffin Tins:
- Preheat the oven to 350°F/175°C
- Spritz each cup of the muffin tin with spray oil or grease with shortening
- Pour the wet ingredients into the dry and beat together until a smooth batter forms
- Divide batter evenly between the muffin cups, filling each cup no more than ½ full
- Bake about 20-22 minutes or until they spring back if touched lightly in the center, they should be golden brown
- Allow to cool for a minute or two in the tin, then loosen the sides of each roll with a knife or other thin implement
- Remove from tin to a wire rack to finish cooling
- Cool completely before storing in an airtight container or ziplock bag with a paper towel at the bottom to absorb excess moisture
- After the first day, store chilled

Buckwheat Rolls

Yields about 24 Rolls

Hearty and wholesome meets moist and tender in these lovely little rolls which feature a light, soft bite and taste equally wonderful slathered with "butter" and jam, split and used as buns for small burgers, or dunked in stew. A great, go-to recipe to round out your evening meal.

Wet Bowl:
- Stir together then set aside to gel
  - **⅓ C (35g) Ground Flax**
  - **¾ C (175mL) Water**

Dry Bowl:
- Sift, discarding any bits of almond too large to go through the sifter mesh
  - **1 C (120g) Almond Flour**
  - **1 C (120g) Buckwheat Flour**
  - **½ C (64g) Arrowroot Starch**
- Add, then whisk all together to thoroughly combine
  - **1 Tb Baking Powder**
  - **1 tsp Xanthan Gum**
  - **½ tsp Salt**

Return to Wet Bowl:
- Beat together well
  - **¼ C (48g) Coconut Palm Sugar**
  - **½ C (108g) Grapeseed Oil**
  - **3 Large Eggs**
  - **½ C (120mL) Unsweetened Almond Milk**
  - **1 Tb (15mL) Vinegar**

Muffin Tins:
- Lightly grease muffin tins with spray oil or shortening
- Pour the wet ingredients into the dry and beat together until a smooth batter forms
- Spoon batter into tins filling each cup only about ½ full
- Allow batter to rest at least 15-20 minutes while you preheat the oven to 350°F/175°C
- Bake 15-16 minutes or until they spring back when pressed lightly in the center and the cracks no longer look wet
- Loosen the sides gently by running a butter knife around the edge of each muffin cup and place rolls on a wire rack to cool
- Cool completely before storing in an airtight container with a paper towel in the bottom to absorb excess moisture

Drop Biscuits

Yields 14-18 Biscuits

Savory and flavorful, these easy drop biscuits are brilliant served along side a fall meal. They're scrumptious dunked in soup, slathered with "butter," or smothered in a GF, dairy free, white gravy. Yes, you heard me, *biscuits & gravy*! One more comfort food reclaimed for Celiacs and special diet victims the world over! For a flavorful twist, consider dropping the thyme and adding a teaspoon or two of onion powder and perhaps a little garlic powder.

Dry Bowl:
- Sift, discarding any bits of almond or oat too large to go through the sifter mesh

     ¾ C (90g) Almond Flour
     1 C (121g) Oat Flour
     ⅓ C (40g) Amaranth Flour
     1 C (128g) Arrowroot Starch
- Add, then whisk all together to combine

     1 Tb Baking Powder
     1 ½ tsp Xanthan Gum
     ½ tsp Salt
     ½ tsp Ground Sage
     1 tsp Thyme

Wet Bowl:
- Whisk together vigorously until the eggs are well incorporated

     ¼ C (55g) Olive Oil
     ¼ C (48g) Coconut Palm Sugar
     1 Tb (7g) Ground Flax
     3 Large Eggs
- Gently whisk in

     1 ¼ C (300mL) Water

Cookie Sheets or Muffin Tins:
- Preheat the oven to 350°F/175°C
- Line your cookie sheets with parchment paper
- If using muffin tins, lightly grease each cup with spray oil or shortening
- Pour the wet ingredients into the dry and whisk together until a fairly smooth, thick batter forms
- Drop batter onto parchment in rounded globs 2-3"/ 5-8 cm apart, portioning the batter to make 14-16 globs
- Divide batter evenly between 18 cups, they will not be more than half full
- Bake 26 minutes or until well risen, nicely browned and springy/firm to the touch, plus 2 more minutes; this recipe is deceptively easy to under bake, so always err on the side of 2 extra minutes once it looks done
- Remove from sheets or tins and cool on a wire rack
- Serve warm, or cooled, but cool to room temperature before storing in an airtight container with a paper towel in the bottom to absorb moisture
- Store chilled after the first day

White Gravy

Yields 2 Cups Gravy

A very satisfying substitute for that old, much beloved milk and flour concoction. This is the one and only recipe where I will affirm that bacon grease really does something. It does add bit more, precious flavor.

Dry Bowl:
- Add, then set aside

> **3 Tb (24g) Arrowroot Starch**
> **2 Tb (16g) Sorghum Flour**
> **⅛ tsp Finely Ground Black Pepper**

Liquid Measuring Cup:
- Measure out, then set aside

> **2 C (475mL) Unsweetened Almond Milk**

Sauce pan:
- Add

> **3 Tb (36g) Palm Oil Shortening or 3 Tb (39g) Bacon Grease**

- Heat over high heat until hot
- Pour the dry ingredients into the hot fat, then whisk in with a roux whisk or fork
- Cook the ingredients until nicely light brown in color, stirring frequently
- Pour the wet ingredients in as soon as the flour is browned, whisking together vigorously
- Continue to simmer over high heat, whisking almost continuously, until thick, about 2 minutes
- Whisk in about

> **⅜ tsp Salt**

- Immediately remove from heat
- Serve while still warm

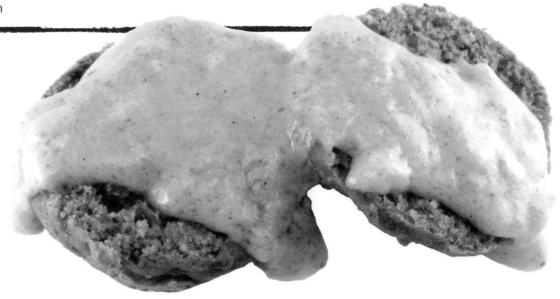

English Muffins
Yields about 16 Muffins

Crunchy-chewy when toasted, replete with nooks and crannies ready to swell with melted Earth Balance or cling to your favorite condiments. These are the ordinary variety, not sourdough, but they sure fix the cravings! Brilliant in the morning for an egg and sausage sandwich. I like to make a bunch, pre-split and freeze them, then I can pop one in the toaster oven anytime I like.

Wet Bowl:
- Stir together and set aside
  - **½ C (52g) Ground Flax**
  - **1 ⅓ C (315mL) Water**

Dry Bowl:
- Sift, discarding any bits of almond too large to go through the sifter mesh
  - **2 Tb (15g) Almond Flour**
  - **½ C (60g) Millet Flour**
  - **½ C (64g) Sorghum Flour**
  - **1 C (128g) Arrowroot Starch**
  - **1 C (192g) Potato Starch**
- Add, then whisk all together to thoroughly combine
  - **1 Tb Baking Powder**
  - **1 ½ tsp Xanthan Gum**
  - **1 tsp Salt**

Return to Wet Bowl:
- Briskly beat in
  - **2 Tb (27g) Grapeseed Oil**
  - **1 Tb (12g) Sugar**
  - **1 tsp Vinegar**
- Stir in gently
  - **1 C (240mL) Unsweetened Almond Milk**
- Pour wet ingredients into the dry bowl and whisk together just until batter is thick and cohesive

Flat Cast Iron or Electric Griddle and Muffin Rings:
- Preheat your pan over medium-high heat, when warm turn down to medium
- Grease your pan an grease your muffin rings and place them onto the pan
- Spoon dough into the muffin rings, smoothing to about ½"/13 mm thick
- Cook 3-5 minutes on the first side or just until the sides begin to look dry, then remove the muffin rings and flip, scooting to a less hot spot in the pan if there is one
- Keep the stove as hot as possible without burning or shortening the cook time, hotter stove equals more nooks and crannies
- Cook 3-5 minutes on the second side or just until the bottom looks done
- Remove to a wire rack to cool
- Re-grease pan and rings before adding more batter
- Split cooled muffins by poking with a fork all around the side making a perforated line, then gently pull open along it

Wraps & Crusts of Righteousness

Wraps

Crêpe Style Tortillas...32

Flat Bread Tortillas...33

Mes Galettes...34

Crusts

Thick Pizza Crust...35

Thin Pizza Crust...36

Pie Crust...37

Compliment

Cobbler Topping for Pies...38

Crêpe Style Tortillas

Yields about 7 Wraps (9"/23 cm)

These tortillas are technically a crêpe that is cooked on both sides, but they make the best burritos, enchiladas and sandwich wraps. They are strong, extremely pliable, with an easy bite and a light but decidedly savory flavor. They also make great quesadillas or stove top tortilla pizzas if you can tolerate cheese or cheese substitutes. They are best enjoyed fresh, within a few hours of making them, but left over batter will keep nicely for upwards of a week. Just cover the bowl with a lid or plastic wrap and pop it into the fridge. When hunger strikes, simply stir well to recombine the separated liquids and grill up as many as you need. This batter in my fridge and canned beans on my shelf are my secret weapons in the battle between feeding hungry kids and keeping tight schedules.

Medium Sized Bowl:
- Sift

> ¼ C (30g) **Amaranth Flour**
> ¼ C (28g) **Quinoa Flour**
> ¾ C (96g) **Arrowroot Starch**

- Add, then whisk all together thoroughly

> 1 Tb (6g) **Ground Flax**
> ¼ tsp **Salt**

- Make a well in center of the flour, then add

> 3 Large **Eggs**
> ¼ C (55g) **Olive Oil**

- Beat the eggs and oil together lightly, then add

> ¾ C (175mL) **Water**

- Whisk all together, taking care to incorporate all of the flour, and beat to form a smooth batter

9" Cast Iron Skillet or Crêpe Pan:
- Warm pan over medium-high heat
- Grease very lightly with spray oil or a minute amount of oil or shortening; be careful not to use too much fat at a time, or the end result will be a greasy, heavy, damp wrap
- Tear off a piece of wax paper a little more than twice as long as your wraps will be and fold it in half, then place on a plate or flat on the counter, you will stack prepared tortillas between the halves of waxed paper to prevent them from drying out
- When the pan is hot, lift it by the handle and while holding it away from the heat, simultaneously slowly pour about ¼ C of batter into the pan and gently tilt the pan to swirl the batter all over the bottom but not up the sides
- Return pan to the heat and continue to cook about 30 seconds or until the edges begin to dry and curl away from the pan
- Using a thin spatula, flip the tortilla, cooking on the opposite side about 15 to 20 seconds or just until the sizzling quiets
- Slip finished tortillas between the layers of waxed paper and cook as many more tortillas as needed for this meal
- Re-grease the pan only as necessary
- Batter may need to be occasionally remixed as ingredients will settle

Flat Bread Tortillas

Yields between 4 Large and 6 Small Tortillas

Expect to use these more as an amazing flat bread than as a typical tortilla. They are tender and soft and simply delicious, but they do frequently split if folded or rolled too tightly. As a tortilla recipe, they are not perfect. But as a flat bread? Just wait until you taste one! This is a deeply, soul satisfying, bread, and miraculously it comes together quickly and simply. For the baking mats, you'll want plain, smooth ones. Mine are from Norpro, but there are many on the market to choose from.

Dry Bowl:
- Sift, discarding any bits of oat or almond too large to pass through the sifter mesh

    ½ C (60g) Almond Flour
    ½ C (60g) Amaranth Flour
    ½ C (64g) Arrowroot Starch
    1 C (121g) Oat Flour
- Add, then whisk together thoroughly

    1 tsp Baking Powder
    ½ tsp Xanthan Gum
    1 tsp Salt

Liquid Measuring Cup:
- Measure out, being careful not to get too much

    ⅔ C (160mL) Water
- Pour this over the dry ingredients and fold together as much as possible
- Knead by hand in the bowl, sprinkling with more **water** only if needed, just long enough to achieve a pleasantly soft, pliable dough
- Separate dough into 4 to 6 equally sized balls of dough, then cover the bowl with plastic wrap to prevent them drying out
- Sandwich 1 ball of dough between 2 smooth, plain silicone baking mats and roll it out between them; you want to roll it as thinly as possible, but you don't want the edges thinner than the body of the tortilla, if they are, roll them back then smooth them out gently
- Either stack rolled out tortillas with waxed paper between them or wait to roll the next out as you cook the first

Heavy bottomed or cast iron pan:
- Heat pan over high heat until warm, but do not grease it
- Once hot, turn the heat down to medium and lay a tortilla into the dry pan
- Cook tortilla for about 60-90 seconds on each side, or just long enough to deeply brown a few small spots
- Cook on the first side again for a few seconds more, just to relax any curling of the edges
- If they are browning too much or too fast, turn the heat down more, this is crucial for softer edges and more tender bread
- Remove cooked tortillas to a plate and cover with waxed paper and a kitchen towel to prevent drying out
- Let them rest at least 3-5 minutes covered before enjoying; they'll be softer and even lovelier

Mes Galettes

Yields about 14 (9"/23 cm) Crêpes

J'aime la galette! Lovely, light, *soft*, buckwheat crêpes are an ages old French staple for a reason. They're so thin and light, accommodate both savory and sweet fillings equally well, and though I think they are perfect when soft and tender, they can crisp up in beautiful, delicate ways too. Cook them with ham and egg on top as soon as they flip for an almost traditional galette complète. Wrap one around a sausage, fill them with baked apples, or even roll them up with peanut butter and jelly! These are a particular favorite of my 5 year old.

Dry Bowl:
- Sift

  ¾ C (90g) Buckwheat Flour
  ½ C (64g) Arrowroot Starch
- Add, then whisk together thoroughly

  2 tsp (8g) Ground Flax
  1 Tb (12g) Sugar
  ¼ tsp Salt

Wet Bowl:
- Whisk together until eggs are well incorporated

  2 Tb (27g) Grapeseed Oil
  3 Large Eggs
  2 C (475mL) Unsweetened
  Almond Milk
- Pour the wet ingredients into the dry and whisk together until well combined
- Cover bowl with plastic wrap or a lid and chill for at least 2 hours or up to overnight
- Remove from fridge and let warm on the counter for 10 minutes or so then whisk the batter together again before cooking

Well seasoned, 9"/23 cm Cast Iron Skillet or Crêpe Pan:
- Lightly grease and set your pan over medium heat to warm
- Cut a sheet of waxed paper twice the size or your pan, fold roughly in half, and lay on a plate or your counter
- When pan is warmed, lift it from the heat and as you pour a scant ¼ C of batter into the pan, tilt it gently in a circular motion to swirl the batter all around the bottom of the pan, but not up the sides
- Return the pan to the heat and reduce it to low; cook just until the edges curl away from the pan and the crêpe lifts free without tearing; sticking is either a sign of needing to cook longer or poor pan seasoning/insufficient greasing
- Flip the crêpe and cook on the second side for 10-20 seconds
- Alternately, for a complète, add toppings as soon as you flip, then fold the sides of the crêpe in toward the center to contain
- Tuck finished, plain crêpes in between the halves of waxed paper to cool and soften, lay a kitchen towel on top if needed to prevent the waxed paper from blowing open
- Fill and serve! Galettes are best fresh but extra batter will keep a few days in the fridge, so just make a few at a time

Thick Pizza Crust

Yields 1 Regular Pizza or 2 Personal Sized

This crust is a bit sticky when rolling it out, but it bakes up lighter and breadier than my thin crust, and won't fold or buckle while eating. It is great for those who love to pile on toppings and don't want them to slide off mid bite.

Wet Bowl:
- Add all, then set aside to gel
  - **½ C (52g) Ground Flax**
  - **1 ½ C (350mL) Water**
  - **2 Tb (27g) Olive Oil**

Mixer Bowl:
- Sift, discarding any pieces of oat too large to go through the sifter mesh
  - **1 C (128g) Arrowroot Starch**
  - **1 C (192g) Potato Starch**
  - **½ C (60g) Millet Flour**
  - **½ C (61g) Oat Flour**
- Add, then whisk all together to thoroughly combine
  - **2 tsp Baking Powder**
  - **1 ½ tsp Xanthan Gum**
  - **1 tsp Salt**
  - **1 Tb Basil, dried or chopped fresh**
  - **½ tsp Coriander**
- Pour the wet ingredients over the dry, then attach a dough hook or similar sturdy attachment to mixer
- Begin mixing on low, gradually increasing in speed to a medium setting, beating until a thick, sticky dough is formed
- If necessary, fold in any left over clumps of flour using your handy silicone scraper or similar

Pizza Pan or Cookie Sheet:
- Preheat the oven to 350°F/175°C
- Cut a sheet of parchment about the size of your pan and lay it out on your counter
- Turn all of your dough out onto the parchment, or if making smaller pizzas, work with half the dough at a time
- Dust a silicone baking mat or sheet of waxed paper with potato starch, then lay it starch side down atop the dough
- Working in as few strokes as possible, roll the dough out to ¼-⅜"/ 6-9 mm thick, then slide the whole thing onto your pan
- Peel off the top mat/paper and prebake the crust only for 14 minutes
- Remove from oven, slide parchment with crust onto cooling rack and top pizza as desired, sliding back onto pan when finished
- Increase oven temperature to 400°F/205°C
- Bake again until toppings look done, anywhere from 15-30 minutes
- Again slide parchment and pizza off of the pan onto a wire rack
- Cool just until toppings are set enough to cut, then slice and serve

For Frozen Pizza:
- After pre-baking crust, allow to cool completely
- Top as desired
- Slide onto a cardboard cake board or cooled pizza pan, wrap well with plastic wrap and freeze
- To heat, unwrap, slide off cardboard (if used) onto pan, and bake as usual until toppings are done

Thin Pizza Crust
Yields 2 Regular (12"/30.5 cm) Pizzas

This crust crisps nicely at the edges while maintaining a fairly tender, pleasant bite. It holds up well under the weight of piled on toppings while remaining pleasingly pliable, and though it's a bit dense, it tastes great. It's even quick to make, with no rise times or other nonsense and it rolls out like a dream with no special tricks or chilling.

Small Bowl:
- Stir together then set aside to gel
  - ¼ C (26g) Ground Flax
  - ⅔ C (160mL) Water

Dry Bowl:
- Sift, discarding any pieces of oat too large to go through the sifter mesh
  - 1 C (121g) Oat Flour
  - ¾ C (96g) Arrowroot Starch
  - ½ C (96g) Potato Starch
  - 2 Tb (15g) Powdered Sugar
- Add, then whisk all together to thoroughly combine
  - 2 tsp Baking Powder
  - 1 ½ tsp Xanthan Gum
  - ½ tsp Salt
  - ¼ tsp Ground Sage
  - 2 tsp Dried Basil (optional)

Wet Bowl:
- Smear together until incorporated
  - ⅓ C (64g) Palm Oil Shortening
  - 2 Tb (24g) Coconut Palm Sugar
- Add contents of the wet bowl and the small bowl to the dry, then cut together until mostly incorporated
- Knead by hand to finish, forming a smooth, cohesive dough, then divide in half

Pizza Pan or Cookie Sheet:
- Preheat oven to 425°F/220°C
- Cut a piece of parchment paper to fit your pizza pan or cookie sheet, but lay it on the counter
- Turn out one half of the dough onto the parchment, cover with waxed paper or a silicone baking mat
- Roll out between the paper/mat to ⅛"/3 mm thick, stopping to uncrinkle the paper or form the edges if needed
- If desired, pinch the edges up to create a raised boarder, this is helpful if you want to top with beaten egg as shown
- Slide the whole thing onto your pan, peeling the waxed paper or mat off only just before putting it into the oven
- Prebake the crust for 8-10 minutes, then remove from oven to a wire rack or other heat proof surface
- Top as desired, almost to the edge, avoid toppings that are still frozen or insanely juicy as they can saturate the dough
- One cheese substitution is to beat 1-2 eggs with a pinch of salt and carefully pour over the pizza as not to let it run off
- Return to oven and bake until toppings look done, this can take anywhere from 15-30 minutes
- Slide pizza, parchment and all, onto wire racks; cool just long enough to be able to cut it without losing toppings

Pie Crust

Yields a Top and Bottom Crust for a 9"/23 cm Pie, or 2 Bottom Crusts for 8"/21.5 cm Pies

Tasty, nicely textured, almost flaky, and sturdy too, this pie crust is just plain good. Don't skip chilling the water and shortening, and always pre-bake as directed, even if your pie recipe says not to.

Small Bowl:
- Measure out, then chill for 30-60 minutes
  - **½ C (96g) Palm Oil Shortening**

Dry Bowl:
- Sift, discarding any pieces of almond too large to go through the sifter mesh
  - **¾ C (95g) Sorghum Flour**
  - **¼ C (30g) Almond Flour**
  - **½ C (64g) Arrowroot Starch**
- Add, then whisk together thoroughly
  - **1 Tb (12g) Sugar**
  - **½ tsp Xanthan Gum**
  - **½ tsp Salt**
- If you have a food processor, pour dry ingredients into it
- Add chilled shortening to dry ingredients and pulse in food processor or cut in with pastry blender, just until the largest chunks of shortening are smaller than pea sized, then add
  - **¼ C (60mL) Cold Water**
- Bring the dough together by pulsing the food processor a couple more times, just until a soft dough forms, or by using a silicone scraper to fold the water in just until it becomes cohesive

Pie Plate:
- Preheat oven to 350°F/175°C
- Lay out a silicone baking mat on your counter, place ½ (for two 8"/21.5 cm pies) or ⅔ (for bottom of 9"/23 cm pie) of dough on it, then lay another baking mat over the top
- Roll out to about 1"/2.5 cm larger than your pie pan on all sides or slightly more, then peel off the top mat
- Lay the crust face down into the pan, then gently peel off the last baking mat, you may need to help it with your fingers in spots, but if it tears or leaves any holes, simply press back together or patch with a little extra dough
- Trim excess from edges, then lay in pie weights or a layer of plain, dry beans to weigh down any swelling air pockets
- Prebake 8 minutes for most baked pies, 10 minutes for juicier baked pies, 15 minutes for no bake pies
- Remove weights or beans and allow to cool at least 5-10 minutes for baked pies or cool completely for refrigerator pies
- Add filling and continue according to your pie recipe
- If using a top crust, roll about ⅓ of dough out between the baking mats to just the size of the pie pan; don't remove the top mat, instead slide the whole thing onto a cookie sheet and slip it into the fridge to chill just while the bottom crust is baking
- After filling the pie, peel the top mat off, lay chilled dough face down on top of the pie, and peel off the second mat, then press the edges of the crust together to seal and cut a few small holes in the top crust to allow steam to vent

Cobbler Top for Pie or Crisp

Yields Topping for 1 Pie, or a (8-9"/20-23 cm) Round or Square Pan of Fruit Crisp

Here's a sweet, tasty and really easy way to dress up a pie, or make a super simple fruit crisp.

Small Bowl:
- Cut together with a fork until well mixed and of a crumbly texture
  - **⅓ C (67g) Dark Brown Sugar, not packed**
  - **3 Tb (36g) Palm Oil Shortening**
  - **⅓ C (40g) Oat Flour**
  - **½ C (60g) Almond Flour**
- Crumble over the top of your unbaked pie and bake according to instructions, *or*

If making a crisp/simple fruit pie:
- Preheat oven to 375°F/190°C
- For crisp, grease well an 8-9"/20-23 cm round or square glass or stoneware baking dish
- For pie, prepare bottom crust according to recipe on page 37
- Remove seeds or pits and thinly slice enough fruit to layer 1-2"/2.5-5 cm thick in the pan, or to slightly overfill your pie crust, about
  - **3-5 Apples or 4-6 Peaches or 3-4 Pears**
- Arrange the slices neatly and evenly in the pan/crust
- Dot and sprinkle them as you layer the slices with no more than a total of
  - **Scant 1 Tb (10-12g) Palm Oil Shortening**
  - **1 Tb (13g) Dark Brown Sugar, not packed**
- Crumble topping over the top of the fruit; if baking a pie, shield the crust with a pie shield or loosely wrapped foil
- Bake about 45 minutes, or until fruit is fork tender
- If the crumbles brown too quickly, simply lay a sheet of aluminum foil loosely on top for the remainder of the bake time

Pancakes & Waffles

Multigrain Pancakes

Yields about 1 Dozen Large or 2 Dozen Small Pancakes

Hearty, rife with whole grains and packed with nutrition, these are good with the usual butter and syrup, or topped with jam. For an extra kick, try adding a heap of cinnamon and a tiny pinch of clove to the dry ingredients.

Dry Bowl:
- Sift

  ¼ C (30g) Buckwheat Flour
  ¼ C (30g) Amaranth Flour
  ¼ C (30g) Millet Flour
  ¼ C (28g) Quinoa Flour
  ¼ C (32g) Arrowroot Starch

- Add, whisking together to thoroughly combine

  ¼ C (24g) Quick Oats
  2 tsp Baking Powder
  ¼ tsp Salt

Wet Bowl:
- Beat together vigorously until mostly uniform in color and you no longer feel drag through patches of honey

  2 Tb (27g) Grapeseed Oil
  2 Tb (13g) Ground Flax
  3 Tb (62g) Raw Honey
  2 Large Eggs

- Gently whisk in

  1 C (240mL) Unsweetened Almond Milk

- Pour into dry bowl and whisk together into a smooth batter

Flat-bottomed Pan or Griddle:
- Cut a sheet of waxed paper almost twice the size of a large plate, fold roughly in half and lay on a plate, set aside
- Preheat your pan or griddle over medium heat
- Once the pan is warm, grease lightly with a little spray oil or coconut oil
- Drop batter about two tablespoons at a time into the hot pan, leaving plenty of room between for pancakes to spread
- Watch for bubbles to cover most of the surface of the pancake, then flip
- Cook on the second side just until browned, this should happen quickly
- Stack finished pancakes on the plate, between the layers of waxed paper, to prevent them from drying out
- Continue cooking pancakes, re-greasing the pan as needed
- Cooled leftovers can be stored in an airtight container with a paper towel in the bottom to absorb excess moisture

Buckwheat Pancakes

Yields about 1 Dozen Large or 2 Dozen Small Pancakes

My absolute go-to recipe for classic, butter and syrup, pancakes. Earthy sweet buckwheat is lightened by oat and fluffed up into a thick, tender cake that's quick to come together and thoroughly satisfying.

Dry Bowl:
- Sift, discarding any bits of oat too large to pass through the sifter mesh
  - **1 C (120g) Buckwheat Flour**
  - **½ C (61g) Oat Flour**
- Add, whisking together to thoroughly combine
  - **2 tsp Baking Powder**
  - **½ tsp Salt**

Wet Bowl:
- Beat together well, scraping the bottom to incorporate the honey
  - **3 Tb (62g) Raw Honey**
  - **2 Tb (27g) Grapeseed Oil**
  - **¼ C (26g) Ground Flax**
  - **2 Large Eggs**
- Whisk in just until mixed
  - **1 C (240mL) Unsweetened Almond Milk**
- Pour wet ingredients into the dry and whisk together until batter is fairly smooth and thick
- Allow batter to rest while you prepare the pan

Flat-bottomed Pan or Griddle:
- Warm your pan over high heat
- Once pan is hot, decrease heat to medium and grease with a spritz of spray oil or a very little coconut or grapeseed oil
- Spoon batter into pan about 2Tb at a time for small pancakes, ¼ C at a time for larger ones, leaving plenty of room between the pancakes as they will spread
- Cook until the edges bubble a little and the bottom is browning, then flip
- Cook on the second side just until it browns well, this shouldn't take long
- Remove finished pancakes to a plate and cover with a sheet of waxed paper to prevent them from drying out
- Continue with the rest of the batter, re-greasing the pan only as necessary
- Serve warm with your favorite butter substitute and some real maple syrup or try with strawberry preserves!

Banana Pancakes

Yields about 1 Dozen Large or 2 Dozen Small Pancakes

Low calorie, light, moist and supremely tasty, these are great just eaten out of hand, even cold. Even better, they make the most divine peanut butter and honey sandwiches! Or top them with chocolate peanut butter for a rich and nutritious treat. A dozen may sound like a lot, but my two small children can gulp down that much in one sitting. I always make a double or even triple batch to feed us and save some for sandwiches.

Dry Bowl:
- Sift, discarding any bits of oat too large to go through the sifter mesh

⅓ C (40g) Oat Flour
¼ C (30g) Millet Flour

- Add, whisking together to thoroughly combine

½ tsp Baking Powder
½ tsp Baking Soda
⅛ tsp Salt

Shallow bowl:
- Mash with the back of a fork or masher, then measure out

1 C (240mL) Mashed Banana

Wet Bowl:
- Add banana and

2 Large Eggs

- Beat together lightly with a fork
- Pour over the dry ingredients and mash together, mixing with the fork until well combined
- Batter should still have small lumps of banana, but no unmixed bits of flour or egg

Flat-Bottomed Pan or Griddle:
- Heat pan over medium-high heat
- When warm, grease with a little

Coconut or Grapeseed Oil

- Drop batter onto the hot pan by the heaping tablespoon full for small cakes, or up to the roughly level ¼ C full for large cakes, leaving room between for them to spread

- Cook on the first side until the edges appear dry and a few large bubbles come to the surface
- Gently flip the fragile pancakes and cook on second side just until the bottom thoroughly browns
- Remove finished pancakes to a plate or wire rack while you cook the rest
- Lightly re-grease your pan after every batch
- Serve warm or cooled
- Store thoroughly cooled left overs in an airtight container in the fridge

Blueberry Pancakes

Yields about 22 Pancakes

Warm, flavorful blueberries take center stage in these thin, tender, lightly colored pancakes. Serves 3-4 adults.

Dry Bowl:
- Sift, discarding any bits of oat too large to go through the sifter mesh
    - **½ C (60g) Oat Flour**
    - **½ C (60g) Millet Flour**
    - **¾ C (96g) Arrowroot Starch**
- Add, whisking together to thoroughly combine
    - **2 tsp Baking Powder**
    - **½ tsp Salt**

Wet Bowl:
- Beat together well
    - **2 Tb (13g) Ground Flax**
    - **2 Tb (27g) Grapeseed Oil**
    - **3 Tb (36g) Sugar**
    - **2 Large Eggs**
- Whisk in gently just until combined
    - **1 C (240mL) Unsweetened Almond Milk**
- Pour wet ingredients into dry and beat until smooth, then stir in
    - **¾ C (111g) Blueberries, fresh or frozen**

Flat-bottomed Pan or Griddle:
- Warm your pan over high heat
- Once hot, decrease heat a little and grease pan with spray oil, coconut oil or shortening
- Ladle batter into the pan 2 Tb at a time, pouring it in a little circle to distribute the berries, allow several inches/cm between pancakes as they will spread quite a lot
- Cook on the first side just until there are bubbles all over and they only look really wet right around the berries, then flip
- Cook on the second side just until lightly browned
- Stack finished pancakes on a plate and cover with waxed paper to prevent them from drying out while cooking the rest
- If they begin to brown on the first side before they are bubbly all over, turn the heat down just a little more
- Eat. Yum!

Fluffy Ginger & Molasses Hotcakes

Yields about 16 Pancakes

Light, fluffy, warmed by ginger and sweet molasses, these hotcakes are a brilliant treat on a cool morning, especially with a buttery spread and real maple syrup. Like most spiced breads, their flavor only improves over time, so left overs are great, too.

Dry Bowl:
- Sift
  - **1 C (120g) Buckwheat Flour**
  - **½ C (60g) Amaranth Flour**
- Add, then whisk together thoroughly
  - **2 tsp Baking Powder**
  - **½ tsp Baking Soda**
  - **¼ tsp Salt**
  - **1 tsp Ground Ginger**
  - **2 tsp Cinnamon**
  - **⅛ tsp Cloves**

Wet Bowl:
- Whisk together until mostly uniform in color
  - **¼ C (26g) Ground Flax**
  - **3 Tb (40g) Grapeseed Oil**
  - **3 Tb (65g) Molasses**
  - **3 Tb (36g) Sugar**
  - **1 Large Egg**
- Whisk in gently
  - **1 C (240mL) Unsweetened Almond Milk**
- Pour all into dry bowl and whisk together just until well combined, batter will be thick

Flat-bottomed Pan or Griddle:
- Warm your pan over medium heat
- Cut a sheet of waxed paper almost twice the size of your plate or serving dish, fold roughly in half and lay on the plate, set aside
- When pan is warm, grease with a little spray oil or coconut oil
- Dollop batter about 2 Tb at a time into the pan, spreading it out a little as you do
- Cook on the first side until puffed and the edges appear to be drying
- Flip, cooking on the second side until even puffier and well browned
- These can brown very quickly, and should be dark, but be prepared to turn the heat down on the stove if they begin to over brown before they can fluff up
- Pile finished hotcakes onto your plate or serving dish between the halves of waxed paper, making sure they are covered to prevent drying out

Swedish Pancakes

Yields about 1 Dozen 9"/23 cm Crêpes

More a crêpe than a pancake, these are thin, tender, and lightly sweet with a hint of vanilla. Serve them with a dollop of your favorite jam, wrapped around juicy, seasonal berries, or enveloping warm, baked apple slices.

Dry Bowl:
- Sift, discarding any bits of almond too large to go through the sifter mesh
  - **½ C (60g) Millet Flour**
  - **1 Tb (8g) Almond Flour**
  - **¾ C (96g) Arrowroot Starch**
- Add, then whisk together thoroughly
  - **¼ tsp Xanthan Gum**

Wet Bowl:
- Beat vigorously to dissolve the sugar a little
  - **2 Tb (24g) Sugar**
  - **3 Tb (40g) Grapeseed Oil**
  - **3 Large Eggs**
  - **½ Tsp Vanilla Extract**
- Gently whisk in
  - **1 ½ C (350mL) Unsweetened Almond Milk**

- Pour over the dry ingredients and whisk together until a smooth, thin batter forms
- Allow batter to rest while the pan warms

Flat-bottomed Pan or Griddle:
- Set the pan or griddle to warm over medium heat
- Cut a sheet of waxed paper twice of your pan, fold roughly in half and lay on a plate or the counter
- Grease pan very lightly with spray oil or a minute amount of shortening
- Lift pan by the handle and while holding it away from the heat, simultaneously slowly pour ¼-⅓ C of batter into the pan and gently tilt the pan to swirl the batter all over the bottom, but not up the sides
- Return pan to the heat and cook about 60 seconds or until the edges begin to dry and curl away from the pan
- Use a thin spatula to flip, cooking on the second side only about 15 seconds or just until the crackling quiets
- Stack finished pancakes between the halves of waxed paper, making sure they are covered to prevent drying out
- Continue to cook one pancake at a time, re-greasing the pan only as necessary
- If pancakes start cooking faster than they should don't be shy about turning down the heat, you want them to stay moist
- Fill or top as desired; these are best enjoyed fresh

Belgian Waffles

Yields about 6 Large Waffles

Everything a waffle should be. This recipe creates *amazing* belgian waffles; barely sweet, moist, airy insides, with crispy, but yielding outsides. They're at their best when baked in a deep pocket waffle iron that flips or turns over to achieve the most airy distribution. Using the right type of waffle iron will significantly improve your results.

DryBowl:
- Sift, discarding any bits of almond or oat too large to go through the sifter mesh

    1 C (121g) Oat Flour
    1 C (128g) Arrowroot Starch
    ½ C (60g) Almond Flour
- Add, then whisk together to make one flour

    1 Tb Baking Powder
    ½ tsp Salt

Mixer Bowl:
- Beat on high until thick and foamy

    3 Large Eggs
    ¼ C (48g) Sugar
- Add, then beat in at medium speed just until incorporated, taking care not to over beat

    ¼ C (54g) Grapeseed Oil
    1½ C (350mL) Unsweetened Almond Milk
    ½ tsp Vanilla Extract
- Pour dry ingredients over wet and whisk together by hand just until thoroughly combined, again avoiding over mixing

Waffle Iron:
- Preheat your waffle iron according to the manufacturer's instructions
- Waffle irons vary, but if yours has a temperature control, a fairly high heat setting is likely needed for this recipe
- Grease your heated waffle iron well with spray oil on top and bottom
- Add enough batter to just fill the bottom of the waffle iron without over filling it
- Close iron and cook according to the waffle maker's instructions, but do not remove waffle until steam slows to a very little
- Carefully remove finished waffles to a wire rack and don't crowd them, this will keep the outside crisp
- Re-grease the waffle iron well before each new waffle
- When cool enough to handle, serve immediately

For awesome, homemade frozen waffles
- Gently stack enough cooled waffles into a ziplock freezer bag to fill it without crushing them
- Lay the bag on a level surface in the freezer or even better, a deep freezer
- Prepare frozen waffles by heating in a toaster or toaster oven, just until crispy and warm

Muffins of Holiness

Apple Cinnamon Muffins

Yields One Dozen Muffins

Oh, the rich, buttery euphoria that is baked apple. I always use a good firm fleshed eating variety of apple in my baking, like Pink Lady or Braeburn. They add a richness and depth to the flavor that Granny Smith just can't rival.

Cutting Board:
- Peel, core and finely dice
  - **1½ C (165g) Firm Fleshed Apples, usually 1 ½-2 whole apples**

Dry Bowl:
- Sift, discarding any bits of almond too large to go through the sifter mesh
  - **¾ C (90g) Almond Flour**
  - **1 C (120g) Millet Flour**
  - **½ C (56g) Quinoa Flour**
  - **¼ C (32g) Arrowroot Starch**
- Add, then whisk all together to thoroughly combine
  - **1 tsp Xanthan Gum**
  - **2 tsp Baking Powder**
  - **1 Tb Cinnamon**
  - **½ tsp Salt**

Wet Bowl:
- Whisk together until uniform in color
  - **⅓ C (72g) Grapeseed Oil**
  - **⅔ C (211g) Maple syrup**
  - **3 Large Eggs**
- Whisk in
  - **⅔ C (160mL) Water**

Muffin Tins:
- Either line muffin tins with paper liners, or grease each cup with spray oil
- Pour the wet ingredients into the dry ingredients and whisk together until a smooth batter forms
- With silicone scraper or similar, fold in the diced apple
- Divide batter evenly between the muffin cups
- Allow batter to rest for 20-30 minutes while you preheat the oven to 350°F/175°C
- Bake about 29-30 minutes or until they spring back if touched lightly in the center; they should be well risen and very nicely browned
- Cool muffins for only 1-2 minutes in their tins, then remove them to a wire rack to finish cooling
- Completely cooled muffins may be stored in an airtight container lined with a paper towel to absorb any excess moisture
- Please note, these muffins like to stick to plain paper liners when warm, but will release normally once completely cool, so plan to serve cooled or use non-stick paper liners like If You Care's

Blueberry Muffins

Yields One Dozen Muffins

This recipe makes lightly sweet, slightly hearty yet surprisingly airy, moist muffins that are chock full of nutrients. They're an absolutely awesome way to start the day.

Dry Bowl:
- Sift, discarding any bits of almond too large to go through the sifter mesh
  - **¾ C (90g) Almond Flour**
  - **1 C (120g) Millet Flour**
  - **¼ C (28g) Quinoa Flour**
  - **¼ C (32g) Arrowroot Starch**
- Add, then whisk together thoroughly
  - **1 tsp Xanthan Gum**
  - **2 tsp Baking Powder**
  - **¼ tsp Salt**

Wet Bowl:
- Beat together until pale yellow and the oil no longer separates, start slowly as the honey will be sticky at first
  - **⅓ C (72g) Grapeseed Oil**
  - **⅔ C (211g) Raw Honey**
  - **3 Large Eggs**
- Beat in
  - **⅔ C (160mL) Water**
  - **½ tsp Almond Extract**

Muffin Tins:
- Either line muffin tins with paper liners, or lightly grease each cup with spray oil or shortening
- Pour wet ingredients into the dry and whisk together until a smooth, cohesive batter forms
- With silicone scraper or similar, fold in
  - **1½ C (222g) Blueberries, fresh or frozen**
- Divide batter evenly between the muffin cups
- Allow batter to rest while you preheat the oven to 350°F/175°C
- Bake about 30-32 minutes or until they spring back if touched lightly in the center, they should be well risen and nicely browned, some of the the tops cracking and the cracks looking a little sugar glossy, but not wet
- Cool muffins for only 1-2 minutes in their tins, then remove them to a wire rack to finish cooling
- Completely cooled muffins may be stored in an airtight container lined with a paper towel to absorb any excess moisture

Banana Nut Muffins

Yields 18 Muffins

These are just sweet enough to feel like you're getting away with something, moist and substantial at once, and completely delightful, even chilled. Great choice in the warm summer months.

Dry Bowl:
- Sift, discarding any bits of almond too large to go through the sifter mesh
    - **1 C (120g) Millet Flour**
    - **1 C (128g) Arrowroot Flour**
    - **½ C (60g) Amaranth Flour**
- Add, then whisk all together to thoroughly combine
    - **2 tsp Baking Powder**
    - **1 tsp Baking Soda**
    - **1 tsp Xanthan Gum**
    - **½ tsp Salt**

Wet Bowl:
- Whisk together well, beating until it becomes fairly smooth, slightly thick and a uniform color
    - **¼ C (50g) Dark Brown Sugar, not packed**
    - **½ C (108g) Grapeseed Oil**
    - **¼ C (79g) Maple Syrup**
    - **3 Large Eggs**
    - **1 tsp Vanilla Extract**

- Add, then whisk in thoroughly
    - **2 C (475mL) Puréed Banana**

Muffin Tins:
- Either line muffin tins with paper liners, or lightly grease each cup with spray oil or shortening
- Pour the wet ingredients into the dry and whisk together until a smooth batter forms
- With silicone scraper or large spoon, fold in until evenly distributed throughout the batter
    - **⅔ C (78g) Chopped Raw Walnuts**
- Divide batter evenly between the muffin cups
- Allow batter to rest while you preheat the oven to 375°F/190°C
- Bake about 18 minutes or until they spring back when touched lightly in the center, they should be well risen and nicely browned, some of the the tops cracking and the cracks looking a little sugar glossy, but not wet
- Cool muffins for only 1-2 minutes in their tins, then remove them to a wire rack to finish cooling
- Completely cooled muffins may be stored in an airtight container lined with a paper towel to absorb any excess moisture

Buckwheat Berry Muffins

Yield 18 Muffins

Hearty but oh, so tender cake hides vibrantly colorful, sweet-tart gems in these amazing muffins. A little lemon juice accentuates the tartness of the berries and tenderizes the dough in one magical swoop. These are very satisfying in the morning, split, spread with a little earth balance and served with a nice cup of tea.

Dry Bowl:
- Sift, discarding any bits of almond too large to go through the sifter
  - **1 C (120g) Millet Flour**
  - **¾ C (90g) Almond Flour**
  - **½ C (60g) Buckwheat Flour**
  - **¼ C (32g) Arrowroot Starch**
- Add, then whisk all together to thoroughly combine
  - **2 tsp Baking Powder**
  - **1 tsp Xanthan Gum**

Wet Bowl:
- Whisk together until palm sugar is dissolving
  - **⅓ C (72g) Grapeseed Oil**
  - **⅓ C (105g) Maple Syrup**
  - **¼ C (48g) Coconut Palm Sugar**
  - **2 Tb (43g) Molasses**
- Add one at a time, beating after each addition
  - **3 Large Eggs**
  - **⅓ C (80mL) Lemon Juice**
  - **½ tsp Vanilla Extract**

Muffin Tins:
- Line muffin tins with paper liners, or grease each cup with spray oil
- Pour wet ingredients into dry and whisk together until smooth
- With silicone scraper or large spoon, fold in until evenly distributed
  - **2c Raspberries (246g) or Blackberries (288g), fresh or fully thawed from frozen**
- Divide batter evenly between the muffin cups
- Allow batter to rest at least 20 minutes
- Preheat the oven to 350°F/175°C
- Bake for about 26 minutes, or until they spring back if touched lightly in the center, some of the the tops may be cracking and the cracks looking a little sugar glossy, but not wet
- Cool for only 1-2 minutes in the tin, then remove to a wire rack to finish cooling
- Completely cooled muffins may be stored in an airtight container lined with a paper towel to absorb any excess moisture

*Variation: For a hearty bran/health type muffin, omit berries and add **1 C (117g) Chopped Raw Walnuts** and a packed **⅔ C (111g) Raisins or Currants** that have been measured, soaked in clean water for at least 10 minutes, then drained. This yields a vey filling muffin that boasts the omega 3s of walnuts, extra fiber and vitamins from the raisins, and is also quite tasty!

Chocolate Chunk Pumpkin Muffins

Yields 18 Muffins

This is one of my all-time favorite recipes! Nutritious, flavorful, with a perfect balance of textures, they are simply divine. They do stick to papers liners when warm though, so use non-stick liners like If You Care's, or plan to serve them well cooled.

Cutting Board:
- Chop well, then set aside
    1, 3 oz (85g) Dark Chocolate Bar, minimum 70% cacao content

Dry Bowl:
- Sift, discarding any bits of almond too large to go through the sifter mesh

    1 C (120g) Almond Flour
    ¾ C (90g) Amaranth Flour
    ¼ C (28g) Quinoa Flour
    ⅓ C (43g) Arrowroot Starch

- Add, then whisk all together thoroughly

    1 Tb Baking Powder
    1 tsp Xanthan Gum
    1 tsp Baking Soda
    1 tsp Cinnamon
    1 tsp Ginger
    1/8 tsp Nutmeg

Wet Bowl:
- Beat together until it becomes a uniform color

    ½ C (108g) Grapeseed Oil
    ¼ C (50g) Dark Brown Sugar
    ½ C (158g) Maple Syrup
    3 Large Eggs

- Add, then beat gently to incorporate
    ½ C (120mL) Unsweetened Almond milk

Muffin Tins:
- Preheat oven to 350°F/175°C
- Either line muffin tins with paper liners, or grease each cup with spray oil
- Pour the wet ingredients into the dry and whisk together into a smooth batter
- Add the chocolate, including the little flakes, and the following, then fold in well

    1 C (245g) Pumpkin, canned or baked and puréed
    ¾ C (88g) Chopped Raw Walnuts

- Divide batter evenly between the muffin cups
- Bake for about 27 minutes or until they spring back if touched lightly in the center
- Cool muffins for only 1-2 minutes in their tins, then remove them to a wire rack to finish cooling
- Completely cooled muffins may be stored in an airtight container lined with a paper towel to absorb any excess moisture

Cherry Muffins

Yields 18 Muffins

When I was first putting together the book, I had a blank page in this section. But the idea of the wasted space drove me nuts. The blank vexed me every time I saw it. Eventually I got fed up, tromped to the freezer and dug through it for something, anything, I could throw into a muffin. Oh, cherries. Oooh, cherries and almond! Another miracle and these scrumptious little puffs of heaven were born. Soft, airy, slightly sweet, with silky, baked-in cherries and the delicate aroma of bitter almond, I loveloveLOVE them! I hope you will too. (Thank heavens for blank pages!)

Cutting Board:
- Quarter and if necessary, pit, then set aside
  2 C (276g) Dark Sweet Cherries, fresh or frozen

Dry Bowl:
- Sift, discarding any bits of almond or oat too large to go through the sifter mesh
  ⅔ C (81g) Oat Flour
  ⅔ C (80g) Millet Flour
  ⅔ C (80g) Almond Flour
  ⅓ C (43g) Arrowroot Starch
- Add, then whisk all together to thoroughly combine
  2 tsp Baking Powder
  ¼ tsp Baking Soda
  1 tsp Xanthan Gum
  ¼ tsp Salt

Wet Bowl:
- Beat together until well mixed
  ⅔ C (211g) Maple Syrup
  ⅓ C (72g) Grapeseed Oil
  3 Large Eggs
- Add, then whisk gently just to incorporate
  ¾ C (180mL) Unsweetened Almond Milk
  1 tsp Almond Extract

Muffin Tins:
- Preheat the oven to 350°F/175°C
- Either line muffin tins with paper liners, or lightly grease each cup with spray oil or shortening
- Pour all the wet ingredients into the dry and whisk together to form the batter
- Fold in the cherries along with any juices that may have run from them
- Divide the batter evenly between the muffin cups
- Bake for about 34 minutes or until they spring back if touched lightly in the center
- Cool muffins for only 1-2 minutes in their tins, then remove them to a wire rack to finish cooling
- Cool completely before storing in an airtight container or ziplock bag with a paper towel at the bottom

Tropical Treat Muffins

Yields 24 Muffins

Inspired by my years living in the Virgin Islands, these sweet, slightly ginger-spicy muffins are brimming with island treasures; banana, pineapple, ginger, cashews, lemon, and of course, the indispensable coconut.

Dry Bowl:
- Sift, discarding any bits of almond or oat too large to go through the sifter
  - **⅓ C (40g) Almond Flour**
  - **½ C (61g) Oat Flour**
  - **1 C (120g) Millet Flour**
  - **½ C (64g) Arrowroot Starch**
- Add, then whisk all together to thoroughly combine
  - **1 ½ tsp Baking Powder**
  - **½ tsp Baking Soda**
  - **½ tsp Salt**
  - **1 tsp Xanthan Gum**

Wet Bowl:
- Whisk together well to disperse the honey
  - **⅓ C (72g) Grapeseed Oil**
  - **½ C (165g) Raw Honey**
  - **¼ C (26g) Ground Flax**
  - **⅔ C (53g) Desiccated Coconut**
  - **3 Large Eggs**
  - **1 Tb Lemon Juice**
  - **Zest of 1 Lemon (2 if very small)**
  - **1 Tb Fresh Ginger, finely grated**
  - **⅔ C (160mL) Coconut Milk**

Muffin Tins:
- Preheat the oven to 350°F/175°C
- Either line muffin tins with paper liners, or lightly grease each cup with spray oil or shortening
- Pour wet ingredients into dry and whisk together until a smooth batter forms
- With silicone scraper or similar, fold in until evenly distributed throughout the batter
  - **1 ½ C (350mL) Diced Pineapple, fresh or thawed from frozen but not canned**
  - **1 C (240mL) Diced Banana, about 2 large, choose ripe fruits, but not overripe**
  - **¾ C (88g) Chopped Raw Cashews, optional, but highly recommended**
- Divide batter evenly between the muffin cups
- Bake about 36 minutes or until well browned and they spring back when pressed lightly in a caky spot
- Cool muffins for only 1-2 minutes in their tins, then remove them to a wire rack to finish cooling
- Completely cooled muffins may be stored in an airtight container lined with a paper towel to absorb any excess moisture

The Blessed Cookies

Drop Cookies

Chocolate Chip Cookies...56

Mocha-Chip Cookies...57

Oatmeal Cookies...58

Coconut Biscuits...59

Snickerdoodles...60

Ginger Dawns...61

Chewy Almond Sugar Cookies...62

Crispy Lemon Crackles...63

Sliced Cookies

English Shortbread...64

Lime Shortbread...65

Biscotti...66

Chocolate Biscotti...67

Cut-Out Cookies

Fudge Cut-Outs...68

Spiced Peanut Butter Cut-Outs...69

Cinnamon Walnut Praline Cookies...70

Decorator Icing...71

Bar Cookies

Brilliant Brownies...72

Luscious Lemon Bars...73

Coconut Cream Bars...74

Chocolate Chip Cookies

Yields about 9 Dozen Cookies

Real Chocolate Chip Cookies! Oh, how I missed them. This recipe works well for that delightful, moist-centered, style of cookie that is so popular, but can also crisp up quite well. They even keep well in the cookie jar. Use the shorter times for moister cookies, longer for crunchier ones. The dough also freezes well for weeks. I really like to bake half and freeze the rest.

Dry Bowl:
- Sift, discarding any bits of almond or oat too large to go through the sifter
  - **2 C (242g) Oat Flour**
  - **1 C (128g) Arrowroot Starch**
  - **½ C (60g) Almond Flour**
- Add, then whisk all together to thoroughly combine
  - **2 tsp Baking Soda**
  - **½ tsp Xanthan Gum**
  - **½ tsp Salt**

Mixer Bowl:
- Cream together on high until fluffy, pausing to scrape sides down as needed
  - **1 C (192g) Palm Oil Shortening**
  - **1 C (192g) Sugar**
  - **1C (200g) Dark Brown Sugar, not packed**
- Reduce mixer speed to low while adding
  - **2 Large Eggs**
  - **2 tsp (10mL) Vanilla Extract**
- Increase mixer speed and beat until once again smooth and fluffy
- Reduce mixer to a stir and add dry ingredients, a little at a time
- Increase mixer speed to high one last time for just a few moments to bring the dough together
- Using a silicone scraper or similar, fold in
  - **1 ½ C (258g) Chocolate Chips**
- If it is hot in your kitchen (around or above 80°F/27°C) place dough in an airtight container and chill for 1 hour

Cookies Sheets:
- Preheat oven to 375°F/190°C
- Line cookie sheets with parchment paper
- Pinch off (or chop with a sharp knife if cold) 2 tsp sized chunks of dough, then shape by rolling gently between your palms to form a little ball
- Drop shaped balls of dough onto the parchment, leaving at least 1 ½"/4 cm between them
- Bake full cookie sheets for 6.5-9 minutes, use the shorter time for chewy middles, the longer time for crunchy cookies
- Rest on the cookie sheets about 1 minute or just until cohesive, then use a thin spatula to transfer to a wire rack to cool
- Completely cooled cookies may be stored in an airtight container
- If using frozen dough, let it warm up on your counter for half an hour before you try to slice and shape the cookies

Mocha-Chip Cookies
Yields about 9 Dozen Cookies

Ah, mocha. Lovely, creamy, bittersweet bliss. Imagine enough silky chocolate for decadence, but not enough to hide the briskness and clarity of the coffee. Now add sufficient sweetness to balance it all and remind you it's a treat, and you've got this cookie. The dough can be chilled for days or frozen for weeks before baking, so tuck a little away for unexpected guests.

Dry Bowl:
- Sift, discarding any bits of almond or oat too large to go through the sifter mesh
  - **2 C (242g) Oat Flour**
  - **1 C (128g) Arrowroot Starch**
  - **½ C (60g) Almond Flour**
  - **2 Tb (11g) Natural Cocoa Powder, not Dutched**
- Add, then whisk all together to thoroughly combine
  - **1Tb Baking Soda**
  - **½ tsp Xanthan Gum**
  - **½ tsp Salt**

Mixer Bowl:

- Cream together on high until fluffy and increased in volume, scraping sides down as needed
  - **1 C (192g) Palm Oil Shortening**
  - **1 C (192g) Sugar**
  - **1C (200g) Dark Brown Sugar, not packed**
  - **¼ C (22g) Instant Coffee, regular or decaf**
  - **1 Tb (15mL) Unsweetened Almond Milk**
- Reduce mixer speed to medium and add
  - **2 Large Eggs**
  - **1 Tb (15mL) Vanilla Extract**
- Beat on high until once again smooth and fluffy
- Reduce mixer speed to a stir and add dry ingredients a little at a time until all are incorporated, again pausing to scrape down sides as needed, then kick it up to high just until a nice smooth dough is formed
- Using a silicone scraper or similar, fold in
  - **1 ½ C (258g) Chocolate Chips**
- Wrap the dough in waxed paper, slip into an airtight container, and chill for at least 1 hour before baking

Cookie Sheet:
- Preheat oven to 375°F/190°C
- Line a cookie sheet with parchment paper
- With a sharp knife, chop cold dough into 2 tsp sized cubes, then roll each one between your palms to make little balls
- Drop shaped balls of dough onto the parchment at least 1 ½"/4 cm apart
- Bake 6.5 minutes for moist, chewy cookies, up to 9 minutes for crispier cookies
- Rest on the cookie sheets about 1 minute or just until cohesive, then use a thin spatula to transfer to a wire rack to cool l
- Completely cooled cookies may be stored in an airtight container

Oatmeal Cookies

Yields about 7 Dozen Plain or 10 Dozen with Optional Ingredients

Hearty, toothsome and cinnamon-y sweet, I especially love the apple variation of these cookies. The baked apple chunks add buttery rich flavor and silky moisture that are simply irresistible.

DryBowl:
- Sift

    ¾ C (95g) **Sorghum Flour**
    ¾ C (90g) **Millet Flour**
- Add, then whisk together thoroughly

    1 tsp **Baking Soda**
    1 tsp **Salt**
    2 tsp **Cinnamon**
    ½ tsp **Xanthan Gum**

Plain

With Apple

Wet Bowl:
- Cream together until almost smooth, stopping to scrape down sides as needed

    ¾ C (144g) **Palm Oil Shortening**
    1½ C (300g) **Dark Brown Sugar, not packed**
- Beat in until almost fluffy

    2 **Large Eggs**
    1 tsp **Vanilla Extract**
- Slow mixer to a stir and add the dry ingredients, mixing until smooth, then fold in well

    3 C (288g) **Quick Cook Oats**

Optionally:
- Also fold in

    ¾ C (124g) **Raisins, soaked in water for at least 10 minutes, then drained**
    ¾ C (88g) **Chopped Raw Walnuts**
    -OR- 2 C (220g) **Apple, peeled, cored and finely diced**

Cookie Sheets:
- Cover and pop the dough into the fridge for at least 1 hour (not in the freezer, this is about time more than temperature)
- Preheat oven to 425°F/220°C, or for apple cookies, to 375°F/190°C
- Line your cookie sheets with parchment paper
- Drop dough by about the tablespoon full onto the parchment about 1"/2.5 cm apart
- If desired, flatten the cookies a little with the back of the spoon, this will promote a crispier edge and less densely moist center - purely a matter of personal taste
- Bake 7-7 ½ minutes, or 13 minutes for apple cookies
- Cool on the cookie sheet for about 2 minutes before transferring to a wire rack to cool completely
- Cool to room temperature before storing in an airtight container

Coconut Biscuits

Yields about 8 Dozen Cookies

These crisp edged, chewy centered, little cookies feel delicate and lacy, yet are hearty on the palate and pleasantly filling thanks to the fiber-filled coconut. Though not as uniformly crisp as an English biscuit, these make a lovely accompaniment to a cup of afternoon tea. They are not too sweet to enjoy frequently and have a lovely, delicately coconut flavor.

Dry Bowl:
- Sift, discarding any bits of almond too large to go through the sifter mesh

    1 C (120g) Millet Flour
    ½ C (60g) Almond Flour
    ½ C (64g) Arrowroot Starch
    ½ C (60g) Powdered Sugar
- Add, then whisk all together to thoroughly combine

    2 tsp Baking Powder
    ⅛ tsp Salt

Wet Bowl:
- Cream together with a silicone scraper or similar, you may use a mixer, but is not necessary

    ⅔ C (128g) Palm Oil Shortening
    ⅔ C (128g) Coconut Palm Sugar
- Beat in

    2 Large Eggs
    1 tsp Coconut Extract
- Add the dry ingredients and gently mix them in until a smooth but sticky dough forms
- Fold in

    1 C (80g) Desiccated Coconut
- Wrap dough in waxed paper and slip into an airtight container or ziplock bag
- Chill for at least 1 hour, or up to several days

Cookie Sheet:
- Preheat the oven to 375°F/190°C
- Line cookie sheets with parchment paper
- Scoop up rounded teaspoon to level tablespoon sized bits of dough and gently roll each into a ball between your palms, they will be a little sticky, this is as it should be
- Place balls onto the parchment at least 2-3"/5-7.5 cm apart as these will spread quite a bit
- Bake full cookie sheets for 7-8 min or until deeply golden in color with darker edges
- Cool 1-2 minutes on cookie sheet before using a thin spatula to move them onto wire racks to finish cooling
- Completely cooled cookies may be stored in an airtight container

Snickerdoodles

Yields 5-6 Dozen Small Cookies

These delightful, chewy, cinnamon-sugar cookies have universal appeal. Children love them and adults gobble them up just as readily. For a more grown up treat, try baking them a little longer to crisp them up, then dip them in your coffee. Heaven!

Dry Bowl:
•Sift, discarding any bits of almond or oat too large to go through the sifter mesh

¼ C (30g) Almond Flour
¾ C (91g) Oat Flour
¾ C (96g) Arrowroot Starch

•Add, then whisk all together to thoroughly combine

1 tsp Baking Soda
½ tsp Cream of Tartar
½ tsp Xanthan Gum
¼ tsp Salt

Mixer Bowl:
•Cream together on high, pausing to scrape down the sides as needed, until slightly increased in volume, the brown sugar will still appear grainy

½ C (96g) Palm Oil Shortening
½ C (96g) Sugar
⅓ C (67g) Dark Brown Sugar, not packed

•Slow mixer to a stir and add

1 Large Egg

•Beat until thoroughly incorporated and becoming fluffy
•Slow mixer to low and add dry ingredients a little at a time, then beat until cohesive, scraping down the sides and bottom at least once
•Wrap dough in waxed paper and slip into an airtight container
•Chill for at least 1 hour, or up to several days (Note: chilling creates the classic, chewy center texture of a snickerdoodle, do not skip unless you want completely crunchy cookies)

Cookie Sheets:
• Preheat oven to 350°F/175°C
• Line cookie sheets with parchment
• In a small bowl mix together well

3Tb (36g) Sugar
1Tb Cinnamon

• Pinch off gumball-sized chunks of dough, rolling each one between your palms to make nice, round, little balls
• Drop each ball into the cinnamon-sugar, roll to coat, then place on the parchment, leaving at least 1"/2.5 cm between balls
• Bake full cookie sheets for 6.5 to 7 minutes
• Immediately remove baked cookies to a cooling rack using a thin spatula
• When completely cooled, those you manage not to gobble up may be stored in an airtight container

Ginger Dawns

Yields about 10 Dozen Small Cookies

These peppy little treats are named for the sunrise. They are moist-crisp, and have a bright, lively spice to them that is neither hot nor syrupy. Unlike traditional ginger snaps, which are usually heavy with the flavor of molasses, these stay light and bright thanks to the brilliant combination of raw honey and cardamom. For the tantalizing play of sun against snow, try serving these spice-warmed cookies with a little frosty, GF, dairy free, vanilla ice cream!

Dry Bowl:
• Sift

1 C plus 2 Tb (135g) Millet Flour
1 C (128g) Arrowroot Starch
½ C (60g) Amaranth Flour
• Add, then whisk all together to thoroughly combine
2 tsp Baking soda
1 tsp Xanthan Gum
2 tsp Ginger
½ tsp Cardamom
¼ tsp Clove
½ tsp Salt

Wet Bowl:
• Cream together, beating until fluffy, pausing to scrape down the sides as needed
¾ C (144g) Palm Oil Shortening
½ C (96g) Sugar
½ C (100g) Dark Brown Sugar, not packed
3 Tb (62g) Raw Honey
• Add, again beating until fluffy
1 Large Egg
• Mix in contents of dry bowl, beating just until a smooth dough forms
• Dough may be used immediately or chilled, well covered, for up to a couple of days

Cookie Sheets:
• Preheat the oven to 375°F/190°C
• Line your cookie sheets with parchment paper
• Into a small bowl, pour about
½ C (96g) Sugar or Sanding Sugar
• Pinch off bits of dough and roll into balls about ¾-1"/2-2.5 cm in diameter but no bigger
• Drop shaped balls into the sugar, roll them around to coat, then place them on the parchment at least 2"/5 cm apart
• Bake for about 7½-8 minutes per batch
• Cool 1-2 minutes on cookie sheet before using a thin spatula to move them onto wire racks to finish cooling
• Cool completely before storing in an airtight container

Chewy Almond Sugar Cookies

Yields about 3-4 Dozen Small or 2 Dozen Medium Sized Cookies

Rolled in sanding sugar, decorated with icing (though that's a little too sweet for me) or just plain, these chewy cookies are a nice, basic recipe that kids love.

Dry Bowl:
- Sift, discarding any bits of almond too large to pass through the sifter mesh
    1 C (120g) Almond Flour
    1 C (120g) Powdered Sugar
    ⅔ C (85g) Arrowroot Starch
- Add, then whisk together thoroughly
    1 tsp Baking Powder
    1 tsp Xanthan Gum
    ¼ tsp Salt

Mixer Bowl:
- Cream together until fluffy, pausing to scrape down the sides as needed
    ⅓ C (64g) Palm Oil Shortening
    ¼ C (48g) Sugar
- Beat in just until well incorporated
    1 Large Egg
    1 tsp Vanilla Extract
    1 tsp Almond Extract, optional
- Slow mixer to a stir and add dry ingredients a little at a time
- Scrape down the sides if needed, then increase the mixer speed, beating just until a cohesive dough forms

Cookie Sheets:
- Preheat the oven to 375°F/190°C
- Line your cookie sheets with parchment paper
- Pinch off either rounded teaspoon or rounded tablespoon sized bits of dough and gently roll each into a ball between your palms
- If desired, roll in
    Sanding Sugar, or any course grained sugar, optional
- Place on cookie sheet at least 2"/5 cm apart as they will spread, flatten balls just a little with the heel of your hand
- Bake 7 minutes for teaspoon sized cookies, 8 minutes for tablespoon sized
- Cool 1-2 minutes on cookie sheet before using a thin spatula to move them onto wire racks to finish cooling
- Cool completely before icing or storing; store finished cookies in an airtight container at room temperature

Crispy Lemon Crackles

Yields about 7 Dozen Cookies

Big air bubbles that form inside these cookies create thin, crispy layers of lightly tart, lemony flavor. Very satisfying to crunch, crunch, crunch, but still just buttery enough to yield pleasantly with each bite. Highly addictive!

Dry Bowl:
- Sift, discarding any bits of oat too large to pass through the sifter mesh
  - **1 ¼ C (151g) Oat Flour**
  - **1 C (128g) Arrowroot Starch**
  - **½ C (60g) Powdered Sugar**
- Add, then whisk together thoroughly
  - **1 tsp Baking Powder**
  - **1 tsp Baking Soda**
  - **1 tsp Xanthan Gum**
  - **½ tsp Salt**

Mixer Bowl:
- Cream together until fluffy, scraping down the sides as needed
  - **¾ C (144g) Palm Oil Shortening**
  - **1 ¼ C (240g) Sugar**
  - **1 Large Egg**
  - **2 Tb (30mL) Lemon Juice**
  - **Zest of 2 Lemons**
- Slow mixer to a stir and add the dry ingredients a little at a time, again scraping down as needed
- Increase mixer speed, beating just until a mostly cohesive dough forms; the dough will be slightly crumbly

Cookie Sheets:
- Preheat the oven to 375°F/190°C
- Line your cookie sheets with parchment paper
- Pinch off generous teaspoon to scant tablespoon sized pieces of dough, roll each one into a ball, than flatten a little between your palms
- Place at least 1"/2.5 cm apart on cookie sheets
- Bake full cookie sheets for 8 minutes or until puffed and cracking and no longer appearing damp
- Cool 1-2 minutes on cookie sheet before using a thin spatula to move them onto wire racks to finish cooling
- Cool completely before storing in an airtight container

English Shortbread

Yields 4-5 Dozen Squares

Sad but true, I have never tasted real English shortbread. And being a Celiac, I never will. So I called in expert assistance, a food-loving friend from the UK, to help me get it right. According to the expert, the taste is right, the texture is right, and she couldn't even tell I hadn't used butter. My whole family gobbles these up as quickly as they can cool.

Wet Bowl:
- Cut together and set aside to gel

    ¾ C (144g) Palm Oil Shortening
    ½ C (52g) Flax, ground

Dry Bowl:
- Sift, discarding any bits of oat too large to go through the sifter mesh

    1 C (121g) Oat Flour
    1 C (192g) Potato Starch
    ½ C (60g) Powdered Sugar
- Add, then whisk together thoroughly

    1 tsp Xanthan Gum
    ½ tsp Salt

Return to Wet Bowl:
- Cut in

    3 Tb (36g) Sugar
    1 tsp Vanilla Extract
- Dump it all into the dry bowl and cut together the best you can, then knead by hand until dough comes together and appears uniform

Cookie Sheet:
- Preheat the oven to 350°F/175°C
- Cut a piece of parchment about the size of your cookie sheet and lay out on your counter or table
- Turn out all dough onto the parchment, place a sheet of waxed paper or silicone baking mat on top, and roll out with a rolling pin to about ½"/13 mm thick

- Peel off waxed paper or baking mat and slide the parchment onto a cookie sheet, dough and all
- Bake 30 minutes, or until the edges just start to brown, it should look set and have ripples like a pond towards the edges
- Cool on the cookie sheet on a wire rack for only about 4 minutes
- Immediately, gently slice into bars with a large, sharp knife; this *must* be done while the shortbread is still very warm
- Slide the shortbread, parchment and all, off of the cookie sheet and onto a wire rack to finish cooling
- Completely cooled shortbread may be stored in an airtight container… if you still have any left by then

Lime Shortbread

Yields about 34 cookies

Zesty, tart, salty and lightly sweet for balance, these pale, flax flecked cookies are quick, easy, vegan, and completely addictive! Serious sour addict? Try increasing the fresh lime zest to a full tablespoon.

Wet Bowl:
- Smear together and then set aside to gel
  - **½ C (96g) Palm Oil Shortening**
  - **3 Tb (20g) Ground Flax**

Dry Bowl:
- Sift, discarding any bits of oat too large to pass through the sifter mesh
  - **1 C (121g) Oat Four**
  - **¾ C (90g) Powdered Sugar**
  - **¼ C (32g) Arrowroot Starch**
- Add, then whisk together to thoroughly combine
  - **½ tsp Salt**
  - **1 tsp Xanthan Gum**
- Begin cutting in wet ingredients with a silicone scraper or fork, then pause to add
  - **1 Tb (15mL) Lime Juice**
  - **2 tsp Fresh Lime Zest**
- Continue cutting together as much as possible
- Finish by kneading by hand until smooth and the dough mostly holds together

Cookie Sheet:
- Preheat oven to 400°F/205°C
- Line cookie sheets with parchment
- Taking half of the dough at a time, roll into a log about 1 ½"/4 cm in diameter
- Slice logs into ⅜"/1 cm thick rounds and place rounds at least 1 ½"/4 cm apart onto the parchment lined cookie sheets
- Bake for about 7 minutes, or until just set and not quite browning yet
- Transfer cookies to a wire rack to cool
- Completely cooled cookies may be stored in an airtight container

Biscotti

Yields about 40 Cookies

Survival food, right? Biscotti was created hundreds of years ago to send to sea with sailors because the well dried, crunchy cookies have a long shelf life. And that is how I justify baking my way through the hurricane season, crisping up batches of this aromatic, divinely flavored, delectable, survival food to dunk in my tea, coffee, or more traditionally, in a glass of wine.

Dry Bowl:
- Sift discarding any bits of oat or almond too large to pass through the sifter mesh
  - **1 ½ C (182g) Oat Flour**
  - **1 C (120g) Almond Flour**
  - **¾ C (95g) Sorghum Flour**
- Add, then whisk together thoroughly
  - **2 tsp Baking Powder**
  - **½ tsp Xanthan Gum**
  - **½ tsp Salt**
  - **½ tsp Cardamom**

Wet Bowl:
- Beat together until well mixed
  - **2 Tb (13g) Ground Flax**
  - **1 C (192g) Sugar**
  - **3 Tb (40g) Grapeseed Oil**
  - **3 Large Eggs**
  - **1 tsp Anise Extract**
  - **1 tsp Almond Extract**
- Pour the wet ingredients into the dry and fold together until it forms an extremely sticky dough
- Fold in
  - **⅔ C (99g) Diced Dried Figs**

Cookie Sheet:
- Preheat oven to 325°F/160°C
- Cut a piece of parchment the size of your cookie sheet and dust it liberally with
  - **Potato Starch**
- Turn out half of the dough onto the parchment, dust hands with starch, and roll into a log almost as long as the parchment
- Repeat with the second half of the dough
- With a starch dusted rolling pin, flatten the logs until they are about ½-⅝"/13-16 mm thick
- With a clean, dry brush, dust away excess potato starch
- Brush a little water across the top of each half of the dough, then sprinkle liberally with
  - **Corse Grained Sugar**
- Slide, parchment and all, onto your cookie sheet, and bake 28 minutes or until firm
- Cool for only 10-15 minutes, then remove to a cutting board and slice each loaf into about ½"/13 mm wide slices
- Lay slices, cut side down, back onto the parchment lined cookie sheet
- Return to the oven for about 22 minutes, or until firm and nicely browned
- Cool finished cookies on a wire rack: completely cooled cookies may be stored in an airtight container

Chocolate Biscotti

Yields about 3 Dozen Cookies

Crunchy, chocolaty, perfect for dunking and not too sweet, these make a blissful compliment to a warm cappuccino.

Dry Bowl:
- Sift, discarding any bits of oat or almond too large to pass through the sifter mesh
  - **1 C (86g) Natural Cocoa Powder, not Dutched**
  - **1 C (120g) Almond Flour**
  - **1 ⅓ C (162g) Oat Flour**
- Add, then whisk together thoroughly
  - **1 tsp Baking Soda**
  - **½ tsp Xanthan Gum**
  - **½ tsp Salt**

Wet Bowl:
- Beat together thoroughly
  - **1 C (192g) Sugar**
  - **2 Tb (13g) Ground Flax**
  - **3 Tb (40g) Grapeseed Oil**
  - **3 Large Eggs**
  - **1 tsp Vanilla Extract**
  - **1 tsp Almond Extract**
- Pour wet ingredients into the dry bowl and add
  - **¾ C (82g) Chopped Raw Pecans**
- Fold all together as much as possible with a silicone scraper or similar, dough will be very sticky

Cookie Sheets:
- Preheat oven to 325°F/160°C
- Cut a piece of parchment the size of your cookie sheet and dust it liberally with
  - **Natural Cocoa Powder**
- Turn out half of the dough onto the parchment , dust your hands with cocoa, and roll it into a log almost as long as the parchment
- Repeat with the second half of the dough
- With a cocoa dusted rolling pin, flatten the logs until they are about ½-⅝"/13-16 mm thick
- Brush a little water across the top of each half of the dough, then sprinkle liberally with
  - **Corse Grained Sugar**
- Slide, parchment and all, onto your cookie sheet, then bake for about 24 minutes or until it feels fairly firm
- Cool for only about 10 minutes, then remove to a cutting board and slice each loaf into about ½"/13 mm wide slices
- Lay the slices, cut side down, back onto the parchment lined cookie sheet
- Return to the oven for about 20 minutes, or until they feel dry and crisp
- Remove slices to wire racks to cool
- Cool completely before storing in an airtight container

Fudge Cut-Outs
Yields about 3 Dozen Medium Sized Cookies

This recipe is richly flavorful, yielding a tender, fudgy cookie that still holds together well, even under the weight of frosting. The dough rolls out easily, is dreamy to work with and keeps its shape when baked. Far, far better than that - a generous dollop of the vanilla version of my Perfect Frosting (page 77) between two of these cookies creates the most *decadent*, bitter chocolate and sweet cream, sandwich cookies of bliss.

Dry Bowl:
- Sift
  - **1 C (127g) Sorghum Flour**
  - **1 C (86g) Natural Cocoa Powder**
  - **½ C (60g) Powdered Sugar**
- Add, then whisk together thoroughly
  - **1½ tsp Baking Powder**
  - **1 tsp Xanthan Gum**
  - **¼ tsp Salt**

Mixer Bowl:
- Cream together on high speed until fluffy, pausing to scrape down the sides as needed
  - **½ C (96g) Palm Oil Shortening**
  - **½ C (96g) Sugar**
  - **½ C (100g) Dark Brown Sugar, not packed**
- Beat in until once again smooth and fluffy
  - **1 Large Egg**
  - **1 Tb (15mL) Water**
  - **½ tsp Vanilla Extract**

- Slow mixer to a stir and slowly pour in the dry ingredients, then stop the mixer and finish folding together by hand

Cookie Sheets:
- Preheat oven to 375°F/190°C
- Line your cookie sheets with parchment paper
- Lay out a sheet of waxed paper or silicone baking mat and turn out no more than half of the dough onto it
- Dust your rolling pin with
  Natural Cocoa Powder
- Roll out dough to about ¼"/6 mm thick
- Cut into shapes with cookie cutters or cut 2-3"/5-7.5 cm shapes with a sharp knife
- Place shapes gently onto parchment lined cookie sheets at least 1"/2.5 cm apart
- Re-roll leftover dough with fresh dough from the bowl and cut more shapes
- Bake full cookie sheets for about 7 minutes or until the cookies are lightly puffed and lose their gloss
- Cool for only 1-2 minutes on the cookie sheets, then quickly and gently transfer to a wire rack to finish cooling
- Cool completely before decorating or storing in an airtight container

Spiced Peanut Butter Cut-Outs

Yields about 5 Dozen Cookies

Creamy peanut butter, warming cinnamon and fragrant clove come together with just a kiss of molasses in these excellent fall cookies that roll out well, cut easily, hold their shapes and are super easy to dress up.

Dry Bowl:
- Sift, discarding any bits of oat too large to go through the sifter mesh
  - **1 C (121g) Oat Flour**
  - **1 C (128g) Arrowroot Starch**
  - **¼ C (30g) Powdered Sugar**
- Add, then whisk together thoroughly
  - **1 tsp Baking Soda**
  - **1 tsp Xanthan Gum**
  - **1 ½ tsp Cinnamon**
  - **¼ tsp Clove**

Mixer Bowl:
- Cream together, pausing to scrape down the sides as needed
  - **1 ¼ C (300g) Pure Peanut Butter**
  - **3 Tb (65g) Molasses**
  - **1 ¾ C (336g) Sugar**
  - **¼ C (48g) Palm Oil Shortening**

- Reduce mixer speed a little and add, beating just until incorporated
  - **2 Large Eggs**
- Reduce the mixer speed to a stir and add the dry ingredients a little at a time
- Increase the mixer speed and beat just until all the dry is incorporated and a smooth dough forms

Cookie Sheet:
- Preheat the oven to 375°F/190°C
- Line your cookie sheets with parchment paper
- Working with ½ the dough at a time, roll out between sheets of waxed paper or silicone baking mats to ¼"/6 mm thick
- Peel off the top sheet/mat and cut into shapes with a 2 ½-3"/5-6 cm cookie cutter
- Place shapes on cookie sheets at least 1"/2.5 cm apart
- Re-roll left over bits of dough with some fresh dough from the bowl and continue to cut shapes
- Optional: using finger tips or a clean paint brush, brush each cookie lightly with water, then sprinkle liberally with
  - **Corse Grained or Sanding Sugar**
- Bake 7 minutes
- Remove to a wire rack to cool
- Completely cooled cookies may be stored in an airtight container

Cinnamon Walnut Praline Cookies

Yields about 3-4 Dozen Medium Sized Cookies

It's difficult to describe the rapture that is this brilliant cookie, but try imagining a buttery, spiced, nut candy, except with a welcoming, tender bite. The dough is easy to work with and holds its shape with only a little spread while baking. Do be certain to use fresh, not stale, nuts. Fresh walnuts in these cookies create basically cinnamon-spiced nirvana.

Dry Bowl:
- Sift, discarding any bits of oat too large to pass through the sifter mesh
  - **1 C (121g) Oat Flour**
  - **1 C (128g) Arrowroot Starch**
- Add, then whisk together thoroughly
  - **1 tsp Baking Soda**
  - **1 tsp Xanthan Gum**
  - **2 Tb Cinnamon**

Blender or Food Processor:
- Blend or pulse until it has the texture of a lightly chunky, nut butter, pausing to stir occasionally, as needed
  - **¾ C (88g) Raw Walnuts**
  - **3 Tb (59g) Maple Syrup**

Mixer Bowl:
- Cream together well, pausing to scrape down the sides as needed
  - **½ C (100g) Dark Brown Sugar, not packed**
  - **½ C (96g) Sugar**
  - **⅓ C (64g) Palm Oil Shortening**
- Add, beating just until smooth
  - **1 Large Egg**

- Beat in the walnut paste until incorporated
- Reduce mixer to a stir and add the dry ingredients a little at a time, again, scraping down the sides as needed
- Beat at a higher speed just until it comes together as a nice, mostly smooth dough

Cookie Sheets:
- Preheat the oven to 325°F/160°C
- Line your cookie sheets with parchment paper
- Cut 2 sheets of waxed paper or use 2 silicone baking mats, lay one on the counter and dust lightly with **Cinnamon**
- Turn half your dough out onto the paper/mat, cover with the second and roll out to about ¼-⅜"/6-9 mm thick
- Cut out shapes with a cookie cutter and place them onto the cookie sheets at least 1 ½"/4 cm apart
- Bake for 9-10 minutes per batch
- Cool only 1-2 minutes on the cookie sheet, then remove them to a wire rack to cool
- Cool completely before decorating or storing in an airtight container

Decorator Icing

Yields about 1 ½ C Icing

Here is a super simple, stable frosting that pipes well and holds its shape. It's also highly adaptable; color it with food coloring, flavor it with extracts, and make it yours, all in around 5 minutes. One batch is enough to slather over 3-4 dozen cookies or pipe plenty of decorations, but to cover and then pipe as on a cake or really fancy cookie, you will want a bigger batch. For topping the Cinnamon Walnut Praline Cookies, I like to substitute 1 Tb Cinnamon for the vanilla extract. Yum!

Dry Bowl:
- Sift

	Single Batch	**1 ½ Batch**	**Double Batch**
	2 C (240g) Powdered Sugar	3 C (360g)	4 C (480g)
	3 Tb (24g) Arrowroot Starch	¼ C + 1 tsp (36g)	6 Tb (48g)

Mixer Bowl:
- Beat on high until fluffy

1 C (192g) Palm Oil Shortening	1 ½ C (288g)	2 C (384g)

- Slow mixer to a stir and add dry ingredients a little at a time, then add

    2 tsp Vanilla Extract
    -OR- ½ tsp Extract or Flavoring, use any you like

- Scape down sides and increase mixer speed to high
- Beat just until fluffy and smooth
- Taste, if desired add more extract ½ tsp at a time, mixing well and tasting after each addition until desired flavor is achieved
- Optionally, add food coloring now, mixing according to the instructions that come with the coloring
- Store extra in an airtight container in a cool spot at room temperature; very shelf stable if not exposed to heat

(Jack-O-Lantern Cookies on pg. 70-71 proudly decorated by Madeline, age 5, and Caleb, age 9; Gluten free sprinkles made in Canada by Fox Run)

Brilliant Brownies

Yields One 14"x9"/35.5 cm x 23 cm Pan of Brownies

Want to feel indulgent? These brownies are the way to do it. Moist, with deep cocoa flavor, fudgy middles and barely sugar-crisped edges, these brownies are utterly brilliant and will not disappoint.

Dry Bowl:
- Sift, discarding any bits of oat or almond too large to go through the sifter mesh

> 1 ¼ C (108g) **Natural Cocoa Powder**
> ½ C (61g) **Oat Flour**
> ¼ C (30g) **Almond Flour**

- Add, then whisk together thoroughly

> 1 tsp **Xanthan Gum**

Mixer Bowl:
- Cream together on high

> 2 C (400g) **Dark Brown Sugar, not packed**
> 1 C (192g) **Palm Oil Shortening**

- Slow mixer and add one at a time

> 4 **Large Eggs**
> 2 tsp **Vanilla Extract**
> ½ tsp **Salt**

- Increase mixer speed; beat until well blended, stopping to scrape down sides as needed
- Again slow the mixer to a stir and add the dry ingredients a little at a time
- Increase mixer speed and beat just until smooth

Rectangular 14"x9"/35.5 cm x 23 cm Metal Baking Pan:
- Preheat oven to 325°F/160°C
- Grease baking dish with spray oil or shortening
- Pour batter into the pan, spreading to an even thickness with your scraper or spoon
- Bake for about 33 minutes or until they've risen and fallen a little and the sugar crust is cracking a bit around the edges, they should look set, even though they will not pass the toothpick test or the spring back test
- Cool in the pan on a wire rack for around 20 minutes to set
- Cut into bars or squares while still warm, wiping the knife clean between cuts
- Store cooled brownies in their pan covered with a lid or plastic wrap or in another airtight container

Luscious Lemon Bars

Yields One 8"/20 cm Square Pan

This is one of those recipes that I don't make very often because I just don't have the restraint to not eat the whole pan myself. The shortbread holds together well and is tasty without being too distracting. The lemon custard top is very lemony, smooth, soft but never thin, and just sweet enough to still embrace a light dusting of powdered sugar. These are truly luscious!

Wet Bowl:
- Cream together then set aside to gel
  - **½ C (96g) Palm Oil Shortening**
  - **3 Tb (20g) Ground Flax**

Dry Bowl:
- Sift, discarding any bits of oat too large to pass through the sifter mesh
  - **1C (121g) Oat Flour**
  - **½ C (60g) Powdered Sugar**
- Add, then whisk together to thoroughly combine
  - **½ tsp Xanthan Gum**
  - **⅛ tsp Salt**
- Add the contents of the wet bowl and cut them into the flour as well as possible
- Finish bringing the dough together by kneading with lightly greased hands; it will be sticky

8"/20 cm Square Baking Pan, any type:
- Preheat the oven to 350°F/175°C
- Plop the sticky dough into the bottom of the pan, lay a sheet of waxed paper on top and use it to press the dough evenly across the bottom of the pan to shape the crust, only allowing it to creep up the sides very slightly
- Bake for 22 minutes, remove and allow to rest for just 1-2 minutes on a wire rack

Medium Sized Bowl:
- While crust is baking, beat together vigorously until yellow and thick
  - **2 C (384g) Sugar**
  - **½ C (64g) Arrowroot Starch**
  - **½ tsp Baking Powder**
  - **4 Large Eggs**
  - **1 C plus 2 Tb (270mL) Lemon Juice**
  - **2 tsp Lemon Zest**
- Pour over the hot crust and immediately return the pan to the oven
- Bake 32-34 minutes or until browned, puffed and set
- Cool in the pan on a wire rack, it will firm up as it cools; do not cut until completely cool
- Dust lightly with powdered sugar just before serving

Coconut Cream Bars

Yields One 8"/20 cm Square Pan of Bar Cookies

A luscious, thick layer of coconut cream rests on a bed of shortbread, blanketed lightly with semi-dark chocolate. Rich and creamy, not overly sweet, and just plain awesome, if you've ever even remotely enjoyed a Mounds, you must try these.

Wet Bowl:
- Cream together, then set aside
  - **¼ C (26g) Ground Flax**
  - **½ C (96g) Palm Oil Shortening**

Dry Bowl:
- Sift, discarding any bits of oat too large to pass through the sifter mesh
  - **1 C (121g) Oat Flour**
  - **½ C (60g) Powdered Sugar**
- Add, then whisk together to thoroughly combine
  - **1 tsp Xanthan Gum**
  - **¼ tsp Salt**
- Add the wet ingredients to the dry, cut together as much as possible, then knead by hand until the dough comes together

8"/20 cm Square Baking Dish, any type:
- Preheat the oven to 375°F/190°C
- Turn the very sticky dough out into your ungreased pan and lay a lightly greased sheet of waxed paper over the top
- Pat down the dough through the paper to form a thick crust covering the bottom of the pan, peel off the paper
- Bake for 8 minutes, then remove to a cooling rack and reduce the oven temperature to 350°F/175°C

Filling Bowl:
- Whisk together until thoroughly mixed
  - **2 C (160g) Desiccated Coconut**
  - **¼ C (48g) Sugar**
  - **¼ C (32g) Arrowroot**
  - **1 Large Egg**
  - **1 (13.5fl oz/398mL) Can of Coconut Milk**
- Pour over the hot crust and return it to the oven for 20 minutes
- Cool in the pan on wire rack to room temperature

Double Boiler:
- Heat gently, stirring often, until most of the chocolate is melted
  - **1 (3oz/85g) Bar of Dark Chocolate, at least 70% cacao, broken into smaller pieces**
  - **½ C (86g) Semi-sweet Chocolate Chips**
  - **2 Tb (24g) Palm Oil Shortening**
- Remove from heat and stir continuously until smooth
- Pour the chocolate evenly over the top of the cooled coconut layer, covering the whole pan evenly
- Chill for at least one hour to set the chocolate
- Once set, cut into small bars with a sharp knife, for the best flavor, allow to come to room temperature before serving
- Store leftovers chilled in a covered pan or airtight container

The Sacred Cakes

Vanilla Butter Cake

Yields Two 8"/20 cm Rounds or about 12 Cupcakes

Each cloud-soft bite of this sumptuous, tender cake almost melts on the tongue like good chocolate. True, it's a misnomer. There isn't actually any butter in this "butter cake," but it is so smooth and moist no one will ever guess. The vanilla is subtle rather than the driving force in the flavor making this an excellent, and far more scrumptious, replacement for the ubiquitous yellow cake. Aching for a less rich, more typical yellow cake? Simply reduce the oil from ¾ C down to ½ C (120mL/108g).

Dry Bowl:
- Sift, discarding any bits of almond or oat too large to go through the sifter mesh
    - **1 C (120g) Almond Flour**
    - **1 C (121g) Oat Flour**
    - **¾ C (90g) Powdered Sugar**
    - **½ C (96g) Potato Starch**
    - **¼ C (32g) Arrowroot Starch**
- Add, then whisk all together to thoroughly combine
    - **1 Tb Baking Powder**
    - **1 ½ tsp Xanthan Gum**
    - **½ tsp Salt**

Wet Bowl:
- Add, then whisk together until the the oil no longer separates and the whole thing turns a pale golden yellow
    - **1 C (192g) Sugar**
    - **¾ C (161g) Grapeseed Oil**
    - **1 Tb (15mL) Vanilla Extract**
    - **4 Large Eggs**
- Add, then whisk together gently until combined
    - **½ C (120mL) Unsweetened Almond Milk**

Cake Pans or Muffin Tins:
- Preheat oven to 350°F/175°C
- For cakes, either cut two rounds of parchment as large as the bottom of your pans and lay inside, or grease pans well with spray oil or shortening
- For cupcakes, either line tins with paper liners, or grease each cup with spray oil or shortening
- Pour the wet ingredients into the dry and beat until it forms a smooth, slightly thick, batter
- Divide the batter evenly between the cake pans/muffin cups
- Bake cakes for about 30-32 minutes, cupcakes for about 26-28 minutes. or until they spring back when pressed lightly in the center
- Cool cakes for 20 minutes on a wire rack before removing them from their pans
- Cool cupcakes for 1-2 minutes in the tins, then remove to a wire rack to finish cooling
- Cool completely before frosting
- For step-by-step instructions on removing cakes from pans without breaking, see page 97

Dawn's Perfect Frosting

Frosts 18 Cupcakes or One Average Cake

My go-to, quick frosting, this stands up well even in warm weather. It is suitable for basic piping techniques and decoration, and develops a delicate crust to protect cakes from drying out, yet maintains a silky, melting texture on the tongue that is pure pleasure. It is sweet, but not offensively so, and the hint of almond extract gives it an aroma and flavor that I just can't get enough of. Switching extracts can create other flavors too. I've done strawberry with 1 Tb homemade extract (see page 97), lemon with 1 Tb juice in place of extract, vanilla by dropping the almond, etc. Just don't add more than 3-4 tsp total liquid per single batch. If you want to both fill and frost a layer cake, and/or do extra piping, I recommend making a double batch.

Dry Bowl:
- Sift

	Single Batch	Double Batch
	3 ¾ C (450g) Powdered Sugar	7 ½ C (900g)
	½ C (64g) Arrowroot Starch	1 C (128g)

Mixer Bowl:
- Beat on high until fluffy, pausing to scrape down the sides and bottom at least once

  1 ½ C (288g) Palm Oil Shortening   **3 C (576g)**
- Add, beating in at medium speed only until well distributed

  2 Large Egg Whites**   **4****
- Scrape down the sides and bottom and mix just a few seconds more
- Stop mixer and add the dry ingredients
- Resume beating on low, gradually increasing to high speed, beating until almost smooth
- Add, then finish beating just until smooth and uniform, scraping down the sides as needed

  2 tsp Vanilla Extract   **4 tsp**
  1 tsp Almond Extract   **2 tsp**
  Optional: Liquid Food Coloring
- Spread or pipe onto completely cooled cakes or cookies as desired

**Please note: Consume raw eggs at your own risk as it does inherently involve a small risk of food-borne illness. To reduce the risk of illness, buy eggs from producers you trust to care for their hens and keep them healthy, only use undamaged eggs with clean shells that have been stored properly chilled, and while cooking, minimize contact between the egg white or yolk and the exterior of the shell.

Yes, I eat them all the time. But no, that does not prove it is a safe practice. Please make your own informed decision about raw eggs and again, consume them at your own risk.

Chocolate Butter Cake

Yields about 18 Cupcakes or Two 9"/23 cm Rounds

I am passionately devoted to this luscious, tender, best-chocolate-cake-ever, recipe. The flavor is smooth and mellow but decidedly chocolate, and will be relished by chocoholics of all ages. It couples happily with either chocolate or vanilla frosting, but the cake is so delectable on its own that frosting is completely unnecessary. It's even super easy to make!

Dry Bowl:
- Sift, discarding any bits of almond or oat too large to go through the sifter mesh
  - **1 C (120g) Almond Flour**
  - **1 C (121g) Oat Flour**
  - **¾ C (65g) Natural Cocoa Powder, not Dutched**
  - **¾ C (90g) Powdered Sugar**
- Add, then whisk all together to combine
  - **1 Tb Baking Powder**
  - **1 ½ tsp Xanthan Gum**
  - **½ tsp Salt**

Wet Bowl:
- Whisk together until the the oil no longer quickly separates
  - **1 C (200g) Dark Brown Sugar, not packed**
  - **¾ C (161g) Grapeseed Oil**
  - **2 tsp Vanilla Extract**
  - **4 Large Eggs**
- Beat in just until combined
  - **⅔ C (160mL) Unsweetened Almond Milk**

Cake Pans or Muffin Tins:
- Preheat oven to 350°F/175°C
- For cakes, either cut two rounds of parchment as large as the bottom of your pans and lay inside, or grease pans well with spray oil or shortening
- For cupcakes, either line tins with paper liners, or grease each cup with spray oil or shortening
- Pour the contents of the wet bowl into the dry and whisk briskly together into a very thick batter
- Divide the batter evenly between the cake pans/muffin cups
- Bake cakes for about 30-32 minutes, cupcakes for about 26-28 minutes, or until they spring back when touched lightly in the center
- Cool cakes for 20 minutes on a wire rack before removing them from their pans
- Cool cupcakes for 1-2 minutes in the tins, then remove to a wire rack to finish cooling
- Cool completely before frosting
- For step-by-step instructions on removing cakes from pans without breaking, see page 97

Silken Chocolate Frosting

Frosts One Double Layer Cake or about Two Dozen Cupcakes

Light and fluffy, satiny-smooth, with a full bodied chocolate taste, this is a favorite among children and adults alike. The flavor is rich and sweet and without the overt bitterness of dark chocolate. It also holds its shape very well and is an excellent choice for piped decorations, but should be used only when it may be welcomed in its natural brown hue, as it is too dark to take color well.

Double Boiler:
- Heat gently, stirring often, until most of the chocolate is melted
  - **1 C (172g) Semi-Sweet Chocolate Chips**
- Remove from heat and stir continuously until smooth, then set aside to cool

Dry Bowl:
- Sift, then set aside
  - **3 C (360g) Powdered Sugar**
  - **1 C (86g) Natural Cocoa Powder, not Dutched**

Mixer Bowl:
- Beat on high until fluffy, scraping down sides as needed
  - **2 C (384g) Palm Oil Shortening**
  - **2 Tb (30mL) Almond Milk**
  - **4 tsp (20mL) Vanilla Extract**
- Slow mixer to a stir, and add in contents of the dry bowl a little at a time
- Stop to scrape sown the sides, then beat briefly on high to fully incorporate the dry ingredients
- Slow mixer once again and pour in the melted chocolate
- Beat on high until again fluffy and smooth and the color is uniform, scraping down the sides as needed
- Spread or pipe onto cakes and/or cupcakes (or if you're like me, sneak a spoon full for yourself, first)

Extreme Dark Chocolate Cake

Yields about 24 Cupcakes or Two 9"/23 cm Rounds

Dark, bittersweet and deeply flavorful, this cake is unforgettable. It takes frostings well and even gracefully accepts the sweetness of Coconut Pecan Frosting to create an unparalleled Extreme German Chocolate Cake. Need even more bitter chocolate? This cake will support up to 1 ½ C (129g) Natural Cocoa Powder, but watch out, that much yields a ludicrously intense cake that desperately needs something sweet (like a lot of coconut milk ice cream) for balance. You've been warned.

Dry Bowl:
- Sift, discarding any bits of almond too large to go through the sifter mesh

> ⅔ C (80g) **Almond Flour**
> 1 C (120g) **Buckwheat Flour**
> ½ C (60g) **Millet Flour**
> ½ C (60g) **Powdered Sugar**
> 1 ¼ C (108g) **Natural Cocoa Powder, not Dutched**

- Add, then whisk all together to thoroughly combine

> 1 Tb **Baking Powder**
> 2 tsp **Xanthan Gum**
> ½ tsp **Salt**

Wet Bowl:
- Whisk together until mostly uniform in color

> 1 ¼ C (250g) **Dark Brown Sugar, not packed**
> 1 C (221g) **Mayonnaise**
> ⅓ C (72g) **Grapeseed Oil**
> 4 **Large Eggs**

- Gently stir in

> 1 Tb (15mL) **Vanilla Extract**
> 1 Tb (15mL) **Lemon Juice**
> ½ C (120mL) **Unsweetened Almond Milk**

Cake Pans/Muffin Tins:
- Preheat oven to 350°F/175°C
- For cakes, either cut two rounds of parchment as large as the bottom of your pans and lay inside, or grease pans well
- For cupcakes, either line tins with paper liners, or grease each cup with spray oil or shortening
- Pour the wet ingredients into the dry and beat together into a fairly smooth, very thick batter
- Divide batter evenly between the cake pans/muffin cups
- Bake rounds for 38-40 minutes, cupcakes for 34 minutes or until cake springs back when pressed lightly in the center
- Cool cakes for 20 minutes on a wire rack before removing them from their pans
- Cool cupcakes for 1-2 minutes in the tins, then remove to a wire rack to finish cooling
- Cool completely before frosting
- For step-by-step instructions on removing cakes from pans without breaking, see page 97

Coconut Pecan Frosting

Frosts and Fills One Double Layer Cake

The classic topping for a German Chocolate Cake is just as tasty without the dairy. This one is a little trickier than most of my frostings because it requires cooking on the stove top, but I think it's worth the effort. The results will be wickedly tasty (if quite sweet) and even better the next day, making it a great choice for frosting a cake that's made ahead.

Dry Bowl:
- Measure out and set aside

> **2 ⅔ C (213g) Desiccated Coconut**
> **1 ⅓ C (145g) Chopped Raw Pecans**

Sauce Pan:
- Add and whisk together gently using a roux whisk if you have one, taking care not to slop it up the sides of the pan

> **1 ½ C (350mL) Coconut Milk**
> **1 ½ C (288g) Sugar**
> **½ C (96g) Palm Oil Shortening**
> **2 Large Eggs**

- Set over medium heat, stirring constantly and gently just until the sugar and the shortening are dissolved/melted
- Continue heating over medium low heat without stirring at all and bring to a simmer
- Simmer for about 5 minutes or until it reaches around 200°F/95°C
- Remove from heat and allow to cool just slightly
- Add the ingredients from the dry bowl and

> **2 tsp Vanilla Extract, optional**

- Fold together until well mixed
- Allow to cool almost to room temperature before frosting
- If stacking layers, allow the bottom layer to set up for 5-10 minutes before adding the top layer

Peanut Butter Cake

Yields 18-24 Cupcakes or Two 9"/23 cm Rounds

These are my cinderella cupcakes. They started out as something grimy and untouchable (cookie recipe utter failure) and then there was this fairy godmother person with almond milk and eggs and this crazy dance number and suddenly we're all dressed up and we're going to the ball! For the record, happily ever after is sweet, tender, and scrumptious with great rise and a beautiful crumb. Don't believe me? Taste some for yourself.

Dry Bowl:
• Sift

> ¾ C (91g) Oat Flour

• Add, then whisk together until thoroughly combined

> **1 Tb Baking Powder**
> **1 tsp Baking Soda**
> **½ tsp Salt**

Mixer Bowl:
• Cream together, scraping down the sides as needed

> **1 ½ C (360g) Pure Peanut Butter**
> **¾ C (144g) Sugar**
> **½ C (96g) Coconut Palm Sugar**
> **2 Tb (13g) Ground Flax**
> **3 Tb (40g) Grapeseed Oil**

• Slow mixer and carefully add one at a time, beating just until smooth

> **3 Large Eggs**
> **1 C (235mL) Unsweetened Almond Milk**

Cake Pans/Muffin Tins:
• Preheat oven to 350°F/175°C
• For cakes, either cut two rounds of parchment as large as the bottom of your pans and lay inside, or grease pans well with spray oil or shortening
• For cupcakes, either line tins with paper liners, or grease each cup with spray oil or shortening
• Add the dry ingredients to the mixer bowl and begin beating on low, gradually increasing mixer speed and scraping down the sides as needed, beating until a nice smooth batter is formed
• Divide the batter evenly between the cake pans/muffin cups
• Bake cakes for 22-25 minutes, cupcakes for about 18-20 minutes, or until they spring back when touched lightly in the center, they will have browned a little and completely lost their gloss
• Cool cakes for 20 minutes on a wire rack before removing them from their pans, for help removing see page 97
• Cool cupcakes for 1-2 minutes in the tins, then remove a wire rack to finish cooling
• Cool completely before frosting

Chocolate Peanut Butter Frosting

Frosts Up To 2 Dozen Cupcakes

Imagine classic peanut butter cups made even more flavorful and rendered smooth and yielding rather than crumbling with each bite. Now obliterate the milk tummy ache that comes afterwards for most of us, and you've got this frosting. It is too dark to take color, and a bit too thick and heavy for fine designs, but takes to larger piping well enough and stands up remarkably well in warm weather, especially when made with Enjoy Life's awesome mini chocolate chips. No matter how you use it, it's a treat in itself.

Double Boiler:
- Heat gently, stirring often, until most of the chocolate is melted
  #### ¾ C (129g) Chocolate Chips
- Remove from heat and stir continuously until smooth, then set aside to cool

Dry Bowl:
- Sift and set aside
  #### 2 ¼ C (270g) Powdered Sugar
  #### ¼ C (32g) Arrowroot Starch

Mixer Bowl:
- Beat together on high until completely blended and gaining slightly in volume, pausing to scrape down the sides as needed
  #### 1 ½ C (360g) Pure Peanut Butter
  #### ⅓ C (64g) Palm Oil Shortening
- Stop mixer and pour in the melted chocolate
- Again beat until thoroughly blended, scraping down the sides as necessary
- Reduce mixer speed to a stir and add the dry ingredients a little at a time
- Scrape down sides and continue to beat just until fluffy
- If intending to spread the frosting, use it while it is soft, then firm it up by chilling the whole cake/cupcakes with frosting on them for 20-30 minutes; chilling allows the melted chocolate within the frosting to set faster and hold its shape
- If too soft for piping, first load bag, then chill it for 10 to 20 minutes before piping
- Conversely, if over chilled, simply rest it on the counter for a few minutes to soften
- Store extra frosting in an airtight container in the refrigerator where it should keep well for weeks
- Chilled frosting will be very firm, but will soften up enough to pipe if allowed to rest on the counter in its container until nearly room temperature

Pound Cake

Yields One Tube Pan or Two Loaves (8.5"x4.5"/21.5 cm x 11.5 cm)

This pound cake is moist, sweet and dense, just as a pound cake should be. The lovely light flavor complements a wide array of toppings (strawberry shortcake anyone?) but is just as delectable on its own. Be especially careful not to over beat this one.

Dry Bowl:
- Sift, discarding any bits of almond or oat too large to go through the sifter mesh

  ½ C (60g) Almond Flour
  ¾ C (90g) Millet Flour
  ¾ C (91g) Oat Flour
  1 C (192g) Potato Starch
  ½ C (60g) Powdered Sugar
- Add, then whisk all together thoroughly
  1 tsp Baking Powder
  1 tsp Xanthan Gum
  1 tsp Salt

Mixer Bowl:
- Cream together until fluffy
  ¾ C (144g) Palm Oil
  Shortening
  2 C (384g) Sugar
- Mix in on low to medium, just until smooth
  1 Tb (15mL) Vanilla Extract
  6 Large Eggs
- Drop mixer to a stir and add
  1 C (240mL) Coconut Milk
- Remaining at a stir, slowly pour in the dry ingredients, mixing just until well combined and no more

Tube Pan or Loaf Pans:
- Preheat oven to 350°F/175°C
- Lightly grease your assembled tube pan or loaf pans with a little spray oil or shortening, not forgetting to grease the center, then pour batter evenly around the center or divide evenly between pans
- Bake about 50-55 minutes or until firm/springy to the touch and cracks no longer appear wet
- Cool in the pan on a wire rack for about 30 minutes
- For a tube pan, loosen the sides with a knife or silicone scraper, then lift the center of the pan out of the sides
- Loosen the bottom and center of the cake as well, then carefully invert onto a plate, remove the bottom of the pan, then re-invert onto a serving dish so that it is once again right side up
- For loaf pans, simply loosen the sides, remove cake from the pan, and finish cooling on wire rack
- Do not slice until cool, as this will improve the final texture, store left overs chilled, well wrapped or in an airtight container

Chocolate Pound Cake

Yields One Loaf (8.5"x4.5"/21.5 cm x 11.5 cm)

A slice of this unadorned cake looks deceptively plain, so that first bite is always a sumptuous surprise. Moist, a little dense, and silky smooth with bitter cocoa played against the sweetness of the cake, it needs no ornamentation to be utterly brilliant.

Small Heat Proof Bowl:
- Sift

⅓ C (29g) Natural Cocoa Powder, must not be Dutch processed

Small Sauce Pan:
- Heat over low heat until hot but not boiling

½ C (120mL) Unsweetened Almond Milk

- Pour hot almond milk over the cocoa powder and stir together into a smooth paste

Dry Bowl:
- Sift, discarding any bits of oat too large to pass through the sifter mesh

1 C (121g) Oat Flour
½ C (96g) Potato Starch

- Add, then whisk all together thoroughly

1 tsp Xanthan Gum
½ tsp Baking Powder
¼ tsp Baking Soda
½ tsp Salt

Wet Bowl:
- Cream together well

½ C (96g) Palm Oil
Shortening
¾ C (144g) Sugar

- Cream in the cocoa paste, then beat in

3 Large Eggs
1½ tsp Vanilla Extract

Loaf Pan:
- Preheat oven to 350°F/175°C
- Either cut a strip of parchment as wide as the bottom width of your loaf pan
  and lay it inside, covering only the bottom and ends of the pan, then grease the sides, or grease the whole pan with spray oil or shortening
- Pour the wet ingredients into the dry bowl and with a spoon or scraper, beat together into a smooth, thick batter
- Pour the batter evenly into the loaf pan and smooth the top
- Bake for about 50 minutes or until well risen and the cracks no longer appear wet
- Cool in the pan for 10 min, then loosen sides, remove from pan, remove parchment if used, and transfer to a wire rack to cool
- Cool completely before slicing or storing in an airtight container

𝕭erry 𝕮ake

Yields Two 9"/23 cm Rounds or 24 Cupcakes

This great, moist, nicely crumbed little recipe is awesomely versatile. It can make cherry, strawberry, blueberry (shown) and probably any number of other lovely, berry-flavored cakes. A little extract really helps to bring out the flavor. Super easy instructions to make your own are on page 97. If desired, food coloring can also be added to the batter just before pouring it into the pan. Please note that bake times are approximate due to variation in the moisture level of the different berries.

Small Sauce Pan:
- Set over low heat and bring gently to a simmer
  ### 2 C (475mL) Puréed Berries or Cherries
- Simmer 5-10 minutes, just until it reduces to about 1 ½ C/350 mL, then set aside to cool

Dry Bowl:
Sift, discarding any bits of oat or almond too large to pass through the sifter mesh
  ### 1 C (120g) Almond Flour
  ### 1 C (121g) Oat Flour
  ### ¾ C (90g) Millet Flour
  ### ¾ C (96g) Arrowroot Starch
- Add, then whisk all together thoroughly
  ### 4 Tb Baking Powder
  ### 1 tsp Xanthan Gum
  ### ½ tsp Salt

Wet Bowl:
- Beat together until roughly uniform in color
  ### 1 ½ C (288g) Sugar
  ### ½ C (108g) Grapeseed Oil
  ### 4 Large Eggs
- Gently whisk in berry purée and
  ### ¼ C (60mL) Unsweetened Almond Milk
  ### 2 Tb (30mL) Homemade Flavor Extract, optional, but highly recommended

Cake Pans/Muffin Tins:
- Preheat oven to 350°F/175°C
- For cakes, either cut two rounds of parchment as large as the bottom of your pans and lay inside, or grease pans well
- For cupcakes, either line tins with paper liners, or grease each cup with spray oil or shortening
- Pour the wet ingredients into the dry and whisk together until smooth and basically uniform in color
- Bake 40-46 minutes for rounds, 28-30 minutes for cupcakes, or until they spring back when touched lightly in the center
- Cool cakes in pans for 20 min, then remove from pan to a wire rack to cool completely, for help, see page 97
- Cool cupcakes for 1-2 minutes in the tins, then remove them to a wire rack to finish cooling
- Cool completely before frosting
- Must be stored chilled after the first day

Lemon Drizzle Cake

Yields One 14"x9"/35.5 cm x 23 cm Cake

Oh lusciously moist, finger-lick sticky, crunchy sugar topped, sweet-tart slice of love. Lemon drizzle, I adore you. Is it even possible not to revel in this cake?

Dry Bowl:
- Sift, discarding any bits of almond or oat too large to go through the sifter mesh
  - **¾ C (90g) Almond Flour**
  - **1 C (121g) Oat Flour**
  - **¼ C (32g) Sorghum Flour**
  - **⅓ C (40g) Powdered Sugar**
  - **1 C (128g) Arrowroot Starch**
- Add, then whisk all together thoroughly
  - **1 Tb Baking Powder**
  - **1 ½ tsp Xanthan Gum**
  - **½ tsp Salt**

Wet Bowl:
- Cream together well to impart more lemon flavor
  - **Zest of 2-3 Lemons**
  - **½ C (108g) Grapeseed Oil**
  - **1 C (192g) Sugar**
- Add, then beat to incorporate
  - **3 Large Eggs**
- Gently whisk in
  - **1 C (240mL) Unsweetened Almond Milk**

14"x9"/35.5 cm x 23 cm Metal Cake Pan:
- Preheat oven to 350°F/175°C
- Lightly grease the bottom of a 14x9 metal baking pan with spray oil or shortening
- Pour the contents of the wet bowl into the dry and whisk briskly together to thoroughly incorporate the dry
- Pour batter evenly into the pan
- Bake for 34 min or until it springs back when touched lightly in the center
- Set it on a wire rack to cool in its pan and immediately begin to make the drizzle

Small Bowl:
- Whisk together until dissolved
  - **1 ½ C (288g) Sugar**
  - **¾ C (180mL) Lemon Juice**
- While the cake is still warm, use a toothpick or similar to poke deep holes into it, all over the surface
- Pour the sugar solution over the cake a little at a time, letting it soak in, and making sure to cover the whole cake
- Allow the cake to finish cooling in the pan and the sugar crust to dry before slicing or storing

Banana Tea Cake

One 10"/25 cm Round Cake

An unconventional tea cake, this one is moist, tender, not-too-sweet and totally delightful, even without any refined sugars. The flavor is mellow, rich without being heavy, and full enough to stand alone beautifully. I like to serve bare slices with a glass of iced decaf as a healthy, utterly delightful, afternoon treat.

Dry Bowl:
- Sift, discarding any bits of oat or almond too large to pass through the sifter
  - **2 C (240g) Almond Flour**
  - **½ C (61g) Oat Flour**
  - **1 C (128g) Arrowroot Starch**
  - **1 C (120g) Powdered Sugar**
- Add, then whisk together to thoroughly combine
  - **2 Tb Baking Powder**
  - **1 ½ tsp Xanthan Gum**
  - **½ tsp Salt**

Wet Bowl:
- Beat together well until thoroughly combined
  - **1 C (192g) Coconut Palm Sugar**
  - **⅓ C (72g) Grapeseed Oil**
  - **4 Large Eggs**
- Whisk in, again until thoroughly combined
  - **2 C (475mL) Puréed Ripe Banana**
  - **2 Tb (30mL) Water**

10"/25 cm Springform Pan:
- Preheat oven to 350°F/175°C
- Take apart your springform and lay a sheet of parchment over only the bottom
- Attach the sides of the springform atop the parchment so that it gets held in place, trim away any excess parchment
- Pour the contents of the wet bowl into the dry and beat together well until it forms a mostly smooth batter
- Pour batter into the prepared pan and gently spin the pan slightly back and forth to level (imagine the movements of a child pretending to drive with a steering wheel, just keep the pan level while you do it)
- If you have a gas oven, lay a sheet of foil on the oven rack, then set your springform on top of it to prevent over-browning the bottom of the cake; if you have an electric oven, you may need to lay a sheet loosely over the top towards the end
- Bake 55 min or until well browned and it springs back and feels fairly substantial when touched lightly near the center
- Cool on a wire rack in the pan for 20-30 minutes, then run a thin knife around the edge to loosen before releasing and removing the sides of the spring form
- Invert the cake to remove the bottom and parchment exactly as you would with any other cake, re-inverting it onto a serving plate to finish cooling, for help, see page 97
- Keeps well at room temperature for a few days, simply line the cut edge with a strip of waxed paper to prevent drying out

Coffee Cake

Yields One 14"x9"/35.5 cm x 23 cm Cake

Piles cinnamon, sugar and nuts, enough to make anything a treat, top this classic coffee cake. Just like the cake I remember from childhood, it's a little dense and only barely moist, all the better to accompany that warm cup of coffee or tea.

Medium Sized Bowl:
- Mash together with a fork until it becomes a well combined, crumbly mixture
        ¼ C (48g) **Palm Oil Shortening**
        ¾ C (150g) **Dark Brown Sugar, not packed**
        ¼ C (30g) **Millet Flour**
        ½ C (59g) **Chopped Raw Walnuts or (55g) Chopped Raw Pecans**
        2 tsp **Cinnamon**

Dry Bowl:
- Sift, discarding any bits of almond too large to go through the sifter
        1 C (120g) **Millet Flour**
        1 C (120g) **Almond Flour**
        ½ C (96g) **Potato Starch**
        ½ C (60g) **Powdered Sugar**
- Add, then whisk together thoroughly
        1 Tb **Baking Powder**
        1 tsp **Xanthan Gum**
        ¼ tsp **Salt**

Wet Bowl:
- Whisk together until uniform in color
        ¾ C (144g) **Sugar**
        ½ C (108g) **Grapeseed Oil**
        1 C (240mL) **Banana Purée**
        ¼ tsp **Almond Extract**
        3 Large **Eggs**

14"x9"/35.5 cm x 23 cm Metal Baking Pan:
- Preheat oven to 350°F/175°C
- Lightly grease your pan with spray oil or a little shortening
- Pour the wet ingredients into the dry and whisk together just until smooth
- Remove 1 C of the batter and mix into it
        2 Tb (25g) **Dark Brown Sugar, not packed**
        1 Tb **Cinnamon**
- Pour plain batter evenly into the pan, then dollop spoonfuls of the batter you added cinnamon to, all over the plain batter
- Drag a knife or scraper gently through the batter in a swirling pattern to swirl in streaks of the cinnamon batter
- Sprinkle the crumbly mixture evenly over the top of the batter
- Bake for about 32 min, or until center is springy and firm
- Cool at least 30 minutes in the pan before cutting, cool completely before storing

White Chocolate Coconut Cake

Yields One Tall Bundt Cake

Rich, silky cocoa butter is gently flavored with coconut and perfectly balanced by a little dark chocolate in this moist, dense cake. It is one of my favorites for entertaining thanks to its simple but lovely presentation and its rich decadence that, while highly indulgent, is never overwhelming.

Small Sauce Pan:
•Melt gently over low heat, stirring occasionally, then set aside to cool

1 C (218g) Cocoa Butter

Small Bowl:
•Mash together with a fork until well mixed and crumbly

⅔ C (53g) Desiccated Coconut
¼ C (48g) Sugar
1 Tb (12g) Palm Oil Shortening

Dry Bowl:
•Sift

1 C (120g) Millet Flour
1 C (192g) Potato Starch
1 ½ C (180g) Powdered Sugar

•Add, then whisk together until thoroughly combined

1 Tb Baking Powder
1 tsp Baking Soda
1 ½ tsp Xanthan Gum
½ tsp Salt

•Also add, no need to mix in

1 C (80g) Desiccated Coconut

Wet Bowl:
•Add melted cocoa butter and cream together with

⅓ C (64g) Palm Oil Shortening
½ C (96g) Sugar

•Whisk in until uniform in color

1 tsp Coconut Extract
4 Large Eggs

•Gently fold in

1 ¼ C (300mL) Unsweetened Almond Milk

Bundt or Tube Pan:
• Preheat oven to 350°F/175°C
• Grease your bundt or tube pan well with spray oil or shortening
• Sprinkle the crumbles from the small bowl evenly over the bottom of the pan
• Pour the wet ingredients over the dry, beating together just until the flour is thoroughly incorporated

- Pour the batter evenly over the crumbles
- Without scraping the bottom, run a thin knife in a swirling pattern through the batter to release any large air bubbles
- Bake for about 60 minutes or until well risen, lightly browned and springy to the touch
- Cool for 30-60 minutes in the pan on a wire rack or similar
- Carefully run a small scraper or knife down the sides and around the center of the pan to loosen
- If using a tube pan, lift the center clear of the sides, loosen the bottom of the pan with a knife, then invert onto serving dish
- If using a bundt pan, simply loosen the cake the best you can and gently invert onto the serving dish
- May be served still warm or fully cooled

Dark Chocolate Drizzle

Drizzle for One Cake or About 1 ¼ C (300mL)

Easy to make, and even easier to love, this thick chocolate sauce offers an ideal, slightly astringent counter to the richness of cocoa butter so prevalent in the white chocolate coconut cake. The drizzle is also awesome over ice cream or anywhere else you might use a great chocolate sauce. Try a little Extreme Dark Chocolate cake, topped with coconut milk Mint Chip ice cream and this. Oh baby! I love to use the Ghirardelli's Unsweetened Bars for this recipe; they flavor the sauce sublimely.

Small Bowl:
- Sift, then set aside
  ### ½ C (60g) Powdered Sugar
Medium Sized, Heat Proof Bowl:
- Break up or chop into smaller pieces before adding to the bowl
  ### 2, 1oz or 4, ½ oz Squares (57g) Pure Unsweetened Chocolate
- Also add, then set aside
  ### 1 C (172g) Semi-Sweet Chocolate Chips
Small Sauce Pan:
- Heat to simmering
  ### ½ C (120mL) Unsweetened Almond Milk
- Pour hot almond milk over chocolate, stirring vigorously until melted and smooth
- Add powdered sugar and continue beating until once again smooth
- Use as a drizzle while it is still warm, as it will thicken as it cools
- I like to drizzle some artistically over the whole cake for presentation, while reserving at least ⅓ to ½ of the recipe to dollop upon each slice as it is served
- Will keep for at least a week at room temperature, longer if chilled
- To thin back out after it thickens, as from chilling, simply warm it gently in a double boiler, or put the container it's in into a hot water bath and allow to sit until partially fluid again, then remove from heat and stir vigorously to smooth out the rest

Rum Cake Reborn

Yields One Bundt Cake

My own spin on the classic, I've used dark and orange rums rather than the usual spiced and given it a lustier allure with anise and vanilla. Don't be put off by the mayonnaise. It's a dairy free substitute for buttermilk or sour cream, and it does a remarkably good job of adding a similar silky moisture and flavor depth. This cake is ultra moist when topped the glaze for maximum rum, and utterly delectable topped with the caramel sauce for maximum flavor. Feeling really crazy? Use both.

Dry Bowl:
- Sift, discarding any bits of almond too large to pass through the sifter mesh
  - **1 C (120g) Almond Flour**
  - **¾ C (90g) Millet Flour**
  - **½ C (60g) Powdered Sugar**
  - **1 ¼ C (160g) Arrowroot Starch**
- Add, then whisk together to thoroughly combine
  - **1 ½ tsp Baking Powder**
  - **1 tsp Baking Soda**
  - **2 tsp Xanthan Gum**
  - **½ tsp Salt**
  - **1 tsp Cinnamon**

Wet Bowl:
- Beat together briskly until uniform in color
  - **1 C (200g) Dark Brown Sugar, not packed**
  - **¾ C (166g) Mayonnaise**
  - **3 Large Eggs**
- Whisk in gently
  - **1 Tb (15mL) Vanilla Extract**
  - **½ tsp Anise Extract**
  - **½ C (120mL) Dark Rum**
  - **¼ C (60mL) Unsweetened Almond Milk**

Bundt or Tube Pan:
- Preheat oven to 325°F/160°C
- Grease your pan well with spray oil or shortening
- Pour the wet ingredients into the dry, whisking together into a smooth batter
- Pour the batter evenly around the center of the pan
- Bake for 45-50 minutes, or until springy to the touch and cracks no longer look wet
- Cool in the pan on a wire rack for about 10-15 minutes
- While the cake is cooling, quickly make the glaze and/or Orange Coconut Caramel Sauce
- When the cake has cooled to just warm, simply loosen the sides and center and invert onto a plate or serving platter

Optional Rum Glaze

Sauce Pan or Small Pot:
- Add, then whisk together gently using a roux whisk if you have one, taking care not to slop it up the sides of the pan

1 C (192g) Sugar
¼ C (48g) Palm Oil Shortening
⅓ C (80mL) Unsweetened Almond Milk

- Set pan over medium heat; continue to whisk it gently together until the shortening is melted and the sugar dissolved
- Heat without stirring until the mixture boils, then turn the heat down to low and continue to boil for 5 minutes
- Remove from the heat and allow to cool just enough for the bubbles to dissipate
- Stand back a bit while you pour in

¾ C (180mL) Orange Flavored Rum or Orange Liqueur

- Whisk together just until fully incorporated

Back to the cake:
- Quickly poke lots of holes all over the cake with a toothpick, skewer or the like
- Pour a little of the glaze into the bundt pan
- Gently return the cake to the pan and begin poking the bottom all over just as you did the top and sides
- Pour the remaining glaze over the bottom and down the sides and inside of the cake
- Allow the cake to soak up the glaze for 5-10 minutes but no longer, then re-invert cake onto serving dish to cool

Orange Coconut Caramel Sauce

Yields Enough to Drizzle Over One Delicious Rum Cake

While not as dark as most good caramel sauces, this sauce is lavishly flavorful. Savor the rich, milky, caramel flavors, the dreamy aroma of coconut, and the brightening accents of orange and salt. It will remain a sauce even when chilled, so drizzle it over anything that tickles your fancy and relish the luxury of fresh, flavorful, dairy free caramel.

Liquid Measuring Cup:
- Measure out then set aside

1 C (240mL) Coconut Milk
¼ C (60mL) Orange Flavored Rum or Orange Liqueur
¼ tsp Salt

Medium Sauce Pan:
- Add, whisking together gently, taking care not to slop it up the sides of the pan

1 ½ C (288g) Sugar
½ C (120mL) Unsweetened Almond milk

- Set over medium heat, whisking gently together just until the sugar dissolves
- Continue heating without stirring until it comes to a boil
- Reduce the heat slightly and boil for 7-10 minutes or until a candy thermometer reads about 270°F/ 130°C and it is a light caramel color; if it begins to get too dark turn down the heat and give it one gentle stir, do be careful not to let it burn
- Remove thermometer, if using, and stand back a bit to avoid being splashed while you carefully and gently pour in the liquid ingredients
- Whisk gently over medium-low heat until all clumps of caramel have melted, then allow to simmer 2 minutes longer
- Remove from heat and allow to cool, stirring occasionally
- Drizzle freely, extra should be stored chilled in an airtight container like a mason jar

𝕶𝖆𝖍𝖑𝖚́𝖆 𝕮𝖚𝖕𝖈𝖆𝖐𝖊𝖘

Yields 24 Cupcakes

A sugar-crisp top crust gives way to soft cake and richly dark flavor, rife with bitter coffee and hazelnut. The darkness is tempered with just enough dark brown sugar to still welcome just a dollop of frosting in the fallen center. These cupcakes are a delightful dance of opposites and like nothing you've ever tasted, all in the most blissful of ways. Note for transparency: Kahlúa has not endorsed or approved this recipe in any way. But they should. It's spectacular.

Dry Bowl:
- Sift, discarding any bits of almond too large to pass through the sifter
  - **1 C (120g) Almond Flour**
  - **1 C (120g) Millet Flour**
  - **1 C (128g) Arrowroot Starch**
  - **½ C (60g) Powdered Sugar**
- Add, then whisk all together thoroughly
  - **1 tsp Baking Powder**
  - **1 tsp Baking Soda**
  - **1 ½ tsp Xanthan Gum**
  - **½ tsp Salt**

Wet Bowl:
- Cream together until fairly well mixed
  - **1 ½ C (300g) Dark Brown Sugar, not packed**
  - **⅔ C (128g) Palm Oil Shortening**
- Beat in until incorporated
  - **⅔ C (57g) Instant Coffee**
  - **4 Large Eggs**
- Gently whisk in
  - **¾ C (180mL) Hazelnut Kahlúa**

Muffin Tins:
- Preheat oven to 350°F/175°C
- Either line muffin tins with paper liners, or grease the tins with spray oil or shortening
- Pour the wet ingredients into the dry, whisking together into a smooth batter
- Pour batter evenly into muffin cups, filling no more than ¾ full
- Bake for 26-28 minutes, or just until the centers no longer appear wet; the centers will have fallen, this is as it should be
- Remove from the pans and cool on wire racks
- Cool completely before frosting or storing

𝔇runken 𝔠oconut 𝔠ake

Yields One Bundt Cake

This is the only cake in the book that I created for my own birthday. Sinfully moist, richly tender, with lingering hints of coconut and the coconut flavored rum that I just can't quite resist, this recipe was motivated by pure desire. It is an idyllic choice for entertaining because it is easy to make, beautiful, delicious and needs no extra toppings or sauces. A note on the rum: to the best of my knowledge, both Malibu and Cruzan Coconut Rum are GF, dairy free, and widely available.

Small Bowl:
- Cut together with a fork until it is well mixed and crumbly, then set aside
  - **½ C (40g) Desiccated Coconut**
  - **¼ C (50g) Dark Brown Sugar, not packed**
  - **2 tsp Coconut Flavored Rum**
  - **2 tsp (8g) Palm Oil Shortening**

Dry Bowl:
- Sift, discarding any bits of almond too large to go through the sifter mesh
  - **1½ C (180g) Almond Flour**
  - **1½ C (180g) Powdered Sugar**
  - **¾ C (144g) Potato Starch**
- Add, then whisk all together thoroughly
  - **4 tsp Baking Powder**
  - **1½ tsp Xanthan Gum**
  - **1 scant tsp Salt**

Wet Bowl:
- Cream together until well mixed
  - **¾ C (144g) Palm Oil Shortening**
  - **1 C (200g) Dark Brown Sugar, not packed**
- Beat in well
  - **4 Large Eggs**
  - **¾ C (180mL) Coconut Flavored Rum**

Bundt Cake Pan:
- Preheat oven to 350°F/175°C
- Grease your pan with spray oil or a little shortening, then sprinkle the crumbles from the small bowl all over the bottom
- Pour the wet ingredients into the dry, whisking together into a fairly smooth batter
- Gently pour the batter over the crumbles, pouring it evenly, all around the pan
- Bake about 40 minutes or until well risen, the cracks begin to look dry, and the cake feels firm when pressed lightly with a finger
- Cool in the pan for 30 minutes, then run a small silicone scraper down the sides and center of the pan to loosen well
- Carefully invert over a plate or serving dish and lift the pan away
- Cool at least 20 more minutes before cutting, and cool completely to room temperature before wrapping or storing

Coffee Frosting

Frosts about 18-24 Cupcakes or One Layer Cake

Like heaven's own café latte! Frost with it quickly or you may find yourself licking a spoon with none left for the cake. Try it between Fudge Cut-Outs, topping a chocolate, banana, or even vanilla cake, or just dolloped on top of some sliced, ripe banana or cooked, ripe plantains. I always make mine with decaf because even my kids go nuts for this frosting. Like most of my frostings, it is stable even in warm weather, silky smooth, and great for basic piping work.

Dry Bowl:
- Sift

5 C (600g) Powdered Sugar
¼ C (22g) Natural Cocoa Powder, not Dutched
½ C (64g) Arrowroot Starch

Wet Bowl:
- Stir together until dissolved

2 Large Egg Whites**
¼ C (22g) Instant Coffee, regular or decaf
2 Tb (30mL) Vanilla Extract

Mixer Bowl:
- Beat on high until fluffy, pausing to scrape down the sides and bottom at least once

1 ½ C (288g) Palm Oil Shortening
- Add the contents of the wet bowl, then beat in at medium speed only just until evenly distributed
- Stop the mixer and scrape down the sides and bottom once again
- Add the dry ingredients all at once
- Resume beating at a stir, gradually increasing to high speed, scraping down the sides as needed
- Beat just until smooth and fluffy and no more
- Frost your completely cooled cakes or cupcakes
- Store left overs in an airtight container; if storing for more than 2 days, store chilled, allowing to come gently back to room temperature by resting on the counter before using

**See Raw Egg Warning on page 77

Most Holy Methods of Cake Removal

Getting layer cakes out of their pans, without breaking

- First, be sure that you use parchment to line your pan, or grease the pan bottom well, then after baking allow the cake to cool for the full amount of time specified in the recipe before attempting pan removal
- Loosen the edges of the cake well with a knife, scraper or similar
- Cover the cake with a tea towel, lay your dominant hand gently atop the covered cake, spread your fingers wide and invert the cake onto your hand
- If you used parchment, simply lift the pan off of the cake and peel off the parchment
- If you greased your pan, grip the pan edge with your free hand and very gently twist the pan, as if you're unscrewing a lid, until the cake releases, then lift the pan free and set it aside
- Again using your free hand, lay a cooling rack or serving dish upside down on top of the upside down cake
- Invert the whole thing once more, you should now have a right side up cake atop a rack or dish, ready to finish cooling

Making Homemade Extracts

If you're concerned about alcohol distilled from cereal grains, can't find good extracts locally, or even if you just don't feel like spending another five bucks every time a recipe calls for flavoring, make your own! It's easy. The only extract I really don't recommend making at home is almond,* but the rest are fair game. Fruit extracts are quick to be ready but less concentrated than store bought; spice extracts are the opposite needing long steeping times but becoming gloriously potent.

Fruit Extracts (non-citrus):
- Choose a small mason jar or similar glass jar with a tight fitting lid (recycled pasta sauce or jam jars are great for this)
- Pack the **Fruit of Your Choice** into the jar fairly tightly, the total amount isn't important except that more fruit = more extract
- Pour enough **80 Proof (40% Alcohol) Light Rum** or equally strong, clear alcohol into the jar to completely cover the fruit
- Close the lid tightly and set in a cool, dark place, mine goes in the cupboard with my plates
- Check on it at least once a day; it's done after brewing for 4 days or once the fruit has lost its color, whichever comes first
- Strain the liquid off into another, clean jar, close tightly and store in the fridge

Spice or Citrus Extracts:
- Choose a glass bottle or jar with a tight fitting lid (recycled pasta sauce or jam jars are great for this, or use the rum bottle)
- Add **1 C (240mL) minimum 80 Proof (40% Alcohol) Light Rum** or equally strong, clear alcohol and a minimum of **3-4 Chopped Vanilla Beans** or **Zest Only of 2-3 Small Citrus Fruits** or **3-4 Cinnamon Sticks** or **¼ C Peppermint Leaves** (dry is fine) or **¼ C Whole Anise Seeds**, use similar ratios for larger batches, e.g. 3 C Rum with at least 9-12 Vanilla Beans
- Close tightly and shake it up, then tuck it into a cool dark place; mine goes under the kitchen sink
- Shake it once a day, as often as you can remember, preferably for at least a month, but allow it to steep at least 3 months
- For vanilla, 6 months of steeping is better, and up to a year is awesome, the flavor of these extracts only improves with time
- Straining into a clean bottle once steeped is important with anise, citrus, and mint, but with vanilla and cinnamon it is unnecessary; I always leave my vanilla pods in the extract indefinitely for richness

*Almond extract is made from bitter almonds, which are extremely poisonous, and almonds that are safe to eat won't produce a good extract flavor, therefore I firmly believe it is best to leave the making of almond extract to the professionals.

Index of Awesomeness

Weight in Grams per US Standard Measurement of Common Ingredients

Flours	Tbsp	¼ C	⅓ C	½ C	⅔ C	¾ C	1C
Almond Flour	8	30	40	60	80	90	120
Amaranth Flour	8	30	40	60	80	90	120
Arrowroot Starch	8	32	43	64	85	96	128
Buckwheat Flour	8	30	40	60	80	90	120
Millet Flour	8	30	40	60	80	90	120
Oat Flour	8	30	40	61	81	91	121
Potato Starch	12	48	64	96	128	144	192
Quinoa Flour	7	28	37	56	75	84	112
Sorghum Flour	8	32	42	64	85	95	127

Nuts & Misc Dry							
Cashews, Chopped	9	36	48	72	95	107	143
Chocolate Chips	11	43	57	86	115	129	172
Cocoa Powder	5	22	29	43	57	65	86
Desiccated Coconut	5	20	27	40	53	60	80
Ground Flax	7	26	35	52	69	78	104
Instant Coffee	5	21	29	43	57	65	86
Pecans, chopped	7	27	36	55	73	82	109
Quick Oats/Oats	6	24	32	48	64	72	96
Walnuts, chopped	7	29	39	59	78	88	117

Sweeteners	Tbsp	¼ C	⅓ C	½ C	⅔ C	¾ C	1C
Dark Brown Sugar	13	50	67	100	133	150	200
Maple Syrup	20	79	105	158	211	237	316
Molasses	22	86	115	173	230	259	345
Powdered Sugar	8	30	40	60	80	90	120
Raw Honey	21	83	110	165	220	248	330
Sugar/Palm Sugar	12	48	64	96	128	144	192

Fats

Fats	Tbsp	¼ C	⅓ C	½ C	⅔ C	¾ C	1C
Grapeseed Oil	13	54	72	108	143	161	215
Mayonnaise	14	55	74	111	147	166	221
Olive Oil	14	55	73	110	147	165	220
Palm Oil Shortening	12	48	64	96	128	144	192
Pure Peanut Butter	15	60	80	120	160	180	240
Shortening	13	51	68	103	137	154	205
Safflower Oil	14	55	73	109	145	164	218

Fruits & Berries

Fruits & Berries	Tbsp	¼ C	⅓ C	½ C	⅔ C	¾ C	1C
Apple, Diced	7	28	37	55	73	83	110
Blackberries	9	36	48	72	96	108	144
Blueberries	9	37	49	74	99	111	148
Cherries	9	35	46	69	92	104	138
Diced Dried Figs	9	37	50	75	99	112	149
Raisins	10	41	55	83	110	124	165
Raspberries	8	31	41	62	82	92	123

Key to the Allergen Chart

All recipes are completely free of gluten, dairy, yeast, rice, beans, tapioca, and gelatin. Enjoy them safely.

✗ Indicates that a recipe calls for the specified allergen, an ingredient containing the allergen, or in the case of the vegan column, is vegan.

❍ Indicates that a recipe can be made free of the specified allergen by omitting an optional ingredient or making a very simple substitution, such as substituting soy or hemp milk for almond milk.

[1] Soy: I have not yet found a good, GF, dairy free, dark chocolate that does not also contain soy lecithin. Dark chocolate is the only ingredient in this book not easily found soy free. Please also note that most mayonnaise contains soy, so if you are avoiding soy, look for a brand without or make your own.

[2] Tree Nuts: Most recipes with the option (❍) to be made tree nut free only contain Unsweetened Almond Milk. To make them tree nut free, simply substitute with unsweetened hemp, flax, or soy milk.

[3] Refined Sugar: These recipes call for either sugar or dark brown sugar. Recipes not marked may still call for maple syrup, raw honey, coconut palm sugar and/or starch, and so are not to be considered sugar free.

[4] GF Oats: Pure, gluten free oats are now widely available; this column is intended to help people with a specific sensitivity to even GF oats. For more information, see discussion of oats on page 11.

[5] Corn: These recipes call for xanthan gum which may or may not contain traces of corn; see discussion on page 13. Xanthan is the only ingredient called for without a 100% corn free substitute. Commercial baking powder often contains cornstarch; use easy recipe for corn free baking powder on page 9. Also see discussion of powdered sugar on page 12.

Allergen Chart

Breads	Page Number	Soy[1]	Peanuts	Legumes	Tree Nuts[2]	Refined Sugar[3]	GF Oats[4]	Corn[5]	Quinoa	Eggs	Vegan
Banana Bread	25			X	X	X	X		X		
Buckwheat Bread	21			X			X		X		
Buckwheat Rolls	27			X			X		X		
Cinnamon Raisin Bread	23			X			X		X		
Drop Biscuits	28			X		X	X		X		
English Muffins	30			X	X		X				X
Gingerbread	24			X	X	X	X		X		
Herbed Bread	22			X		X	X		X		
Oat Bread	20			X		X	X		X		
Small Sandwich Bread	18			X			X		X		
Sweet Dinner Rolls	26			X	X		X		X		
Whole Grain Bread With Oats	19			X		X	X	X	X		
Crusts & Wraps											
Cobbler Topping/Fruit Crisp	38			X	X						X
Crêpe Style Tortillas	32							X	X		
Flat Bread Tortillas	33			X		X	X				X
Mes Galettes	34			O	X				X		
Pie Crust	37			X	X		X				X
Thick Pizza Crust	35					X	X				X
Thin Pizza Crust	36					X	X				X
Pancakes & Waffles											
Banana Pancakes	42					X			X		
Belgian Waffles	46			X	X	X			X		
Blueberry Pancakes	43			O	X	X			X		
Buckwheat Pancakes	41			O		X			X		
Fluffy Ginger & Molasses Hotcakes	44			O	X				X		
Multigrain Pancakes	40			O		X		X	X		
Swedish Pancakes	45			X	X		X		X		

Muffins	Page Number	Soy[1]	Peanuts	Legumes	Tree Nuts[2]	Refined Sugar[3]	GF Oats[4]	Corn[5]	Quinoa	Eggs	Vegan
Apple Cinnamon Muffins	48			X			X	X	X		
Banana Nut Muffins	50			O	X		X		X		
Blueberry Muffins	49			X			X	X	X		
Buckwheat Berry Muffins	51			X			X		X		
Cherry Muffins	53			X		X	X		X		
Chocolate Chunk Pumpkin Muffins	52	X		X	X	X		X	X	X	
Tropical Treat Muffins	54		O	X		X	X		X		
Cookies											
Biscotti	66			X	X	X	X		X		
Brilliant Brownies	72			X	X	X	X		X		
Chewy Almond Sugar Cookies	62			X	X		X		X		
Chocolate Biscotti	67			X	X	X	X		X		
Chocolate Chip Cookies	56			X	X	X	X		X		
Cinnamon Walnut Praline Cookies	70			X	X	X	X		X		
Coconut Biscuits	59			X	X				X		
Coconut Cream Bars	74	X		X		X	X	X	X		
Crispy Lemon Crackles	63				X	X	X		X		
English Shortbread	64				X	X	X				X
Fudge Cut-Outs	68				X		X		X		
Ginger Dawns	61				X		X		X		
Luscious Lemon Bars	73				X	X	X		X		
Lime Shortbread	65				X	X	X				X
Mocha Chip Cookies	57			X	X	X	X		X		
Oatmeal Cookies	58				X	X	X		X		
Snickerdoodles	60			X	X	X	X		X		
Spiced Peanut Butter Cut-Outs	69	X	X		X	X	X		X		

Cakes	Page Number	Soy[1]	Peanuts	Legumes	Tree Nuts[2]	Refined Sugar[3]	GF Oats[4]	Corn[5]	Quinoa	Eggs	Vegan
Banana Tea Cake	88			✗	✗	✗	✗			✗	
Berry Cake	86			✗	✗	✗	✗			✗	
Chocolate Butter Cake	78			✗	✗	✗	✗			✗	
Chocolate Pound Cake	85			○	✗	✗	✗			✗	
Coffee Cake	89			✗	✗		✗			✗	
Extreme Dark Chocolate Cake	80			✗	✗		✗			✗	
Drunken Coconut Cake	95			✗	✗		✗			✗	
Kahlúa Cupcakes	94			✗	✗		✗			✗	
Lemon Drizzle Cake	87			✗	✗	✗	✗			✗	
Peanut Butter Cake	82	✗	✗	○	✗	✗				✗	
Pound Cake	84			✗	✗	✗	✗			✗	
Rum Cake Reborn	92			✗	✗		✗			✗	
Vanilla Butter Cake	76			✗	✗	✗	✗			✗	
White Chocolate Coconut Cake	90						✗			✗	
Frostings & Sauces											
Chocolate Peanut Butter Frosting	83	✗	✗		✗						✗
Coconut Pecan Frosting	81			✗	✗					✗	
Coffee Frosting	96				✗					✗	
Dark Chocolate Drizzle	91			○	✗						✗
Dawn's Perfect Frosting	77				✗					✗	
Decorator Icing	71				✗						✗
Orange Coconut Caramel Sauce	93			○	✗						✗
Silken Chocolate Frosting	79			○	✗						✗
Special											
White Gravy	29			○							○

Made in the USA
San Bernardino, CA
20 August 2014